The Vince Carter Story

BY DOUG SMITH

SCHOL

New York   Toronto   London   Auckland   Sydney
Mexico City   New Delhi   Hong Kong

To my wife, Susan,
for her never-ending love and support;
and our son, Jacob, our pride and joy.

PHOTO CREDITS
NBA Entertainment Photos
Front Cover: Garrett Ellwood. **Back Cover, 7, 72, 74:** Fernando Medina.
4, 8, 76: Noren Trotman. **45:** Jesse Garrabrant. **48, 68:** Nathaniel S. Butler.
53: Andy Hayt. **57:** Scott Cunningham. **61:** Glenn James. **65:** Andrew D. Bernstein.

21, 27, 30, 34, 37: Daytona Beach News-Journal.
40: Jim Hawkins.

13, 14, 16, 19, 23, 29: Special thanks to Michelle Carter-Robinson.

PHOTO CREDITS: INSERT SECTION
I: Andy Hayt. **II:** Andrew D. Bernstein. **III, IV, V, VIII:** Fernando Medina.
VI: Glenn James. **VII:** Noren Trotman.

ISBN 0-439-24106-5

© 2001 by NBA Properties, Inc.
All rights reserved. Published by Scholastic Inc.

12 11 10 9 8 7 6 5   3 4 5 6/0

Printed in the U.S.A.
First Scholastic printing, February 2001
Book design: Michael Malone

TABLE OF CONTENTS

Introduction: Dunkfest...................................4

1. In the Beginning.......................................12

2. Family Ties...18

3. High School Superstar............................26

4. Tar Heels, Here He Comes!....................36

5. Rookie of the Year..................................44

6. Vinsanity, Year 2.....................................52

7. Back to School..60

8. The Future Calls......................................67

Career Highlights..78

DUNKFEST

The buzz that was going through the New Arena in Oakland could be heard hours before the NBA.com Slam Dunk at NBA All-Star 2000 would take place. It had been three years since the contest had last been held, but it was finally back, giving the league's great young stars a chance to show off their acrobatic dunking skills.

For Vince Carter, the weekend was serving as an unofficial coming-out party, and he wasn't about to disappoint his fans. He had recently been overwhelmingly voted into the starting lineup for the Eastern Conference All-Stars, beating out such longtime superstars as Shaquille O'Neal, Grant Hill and Tim Duncan in worldwide fan voting. And in that night's dunk contest, he was the overwhelming favorite. Everyone wanted a piece of Vinsanity.

"I had no idea what to expect," Carter said later, looking back at the contest. He was the first Toronto Raptor to take part in either the dunk contest or the All-Star game. "People can tell you about it and you think you understand, but until you get there and experience it, you really don't know what it's going to be like. You can talk about it all you want, envision it, but until you actually sit there and experience it, I'm telling you—it's a treat."

Carter arrived at All-Star Weekend festivities as the man everyone wanted to see. Shaquille O'Neal made sure to have a courtside seat at the Saturday night dunk contest just to see the player he had earlier called "half man, half amazing."

"I normally don't go to the Saturday night stuff," Shaq said about All-Star Weekend. "But with Vince there, I'll be at the slam dunk. I don't want to miss that."

The dunk contest judging panel, which included Carter's idol and the first great creative dunker, Julius Erving, was thrilled about the upcoming contest. The fans were pumped. "Carter's a superstar now," said one fan from northern China before the contest. "Many say he's the second Jordan. I think he's the first Carter."

It was against that backdrop, with those kinds of expectations, that the young Vince Carter from Daytona, Florida, had to perform. And perform he did.

Vince Carter swears he doesn't practice the dunks that have brought him so much fame. He swears that his creativity is summoned on the moment, partly from the adrenaline that flows before a dunk, partly from the mind of an athletic master. He doesn't name his dunks, like the great Darryl Dawkins did. He just dunks.

As the NBA.com Slam Dunk began, Carter knew he'd have to perform in a way that would separate him from the rest of the field, which included his teammate, good friend and cousin Tracy McGrady, as well as the extremely talented rookie, Steve Francis of the Houston Rockets. It would have to be something spectacular to win—and it was.

One of the rules of the dunk contest was that the

The moment Vince stepped onto the court,
he became one of the NBA's hottest new stars.

Vince Carter's famous slam dunks have amazed audiences across the world.

participants had to perform one dunk aided by a teammate. Carter enlisted McGrady to make a bounce pass just below the free throw line while he took his run-up from center court. Taking the ball on the bounce while he was already in the air, Carter put it between his legs, grabbed it with his other hand, and threw down a vicious one-handed jam that brought the crowd to its feet. Carter had stunned them all.

The judges also saw a windmill dunk that was ferocious. Vince had showed off his strength by jamming his whole forearm into the bucket and hanging on by his elbow. "I've never seen anything like it," marveled Isiah Thomas, one of the judges on the panel. "I've never seen anything like that 360 windmill. It was so creative; it was the best ever."

Carter was just doing what he felt he could. "I had seen something like that in a picture somewhere, I think," Carter said after he completed his awesome dunk. "I just decided to do it right before I did."

It's that kind of creativity that separates Carter from the rest of the pack. Once the spotlight is on him, he delivers like the greats of the game. If there were ever any doubts about his popularity, the events of NBA All-Star 2000 put them all to rest.

The three-day celebration was incredible for the young superstar. Carter was whisked from Toronto to San Francisco on a private jet—he held up the departure so he and McGrady could stop and get some Chicken McNuggets to tide them over on the trip, just like a couple of guys headed off for a weekend vacation. Once the traveling party landed, it was as if Carter was off on one of his fast-break trips down the court—full speed ahead.

There was a photo shoot for the cover of *Sports Illustrated*, more interview sessions, a trip to Oakland, where he made a donation to the Boys and Girls Club to set up a mentoring program, a Team Up appearance for the NBA, and a session with local Toronto reporters where he admitted that the whole weekend was simply overwhelming.

But it was this busy weekend that set up Carter's place in the NBA. It wasn't just because of his dunking or his incredible popularity with fans around the world. Along with the athletic skill that makes him stand out, the personality that few knew before the weekend was finally revealed. He was paid compliments from nearly everyone for the way he handled himself both on and off the court. He impressed teammates, coaches and opponents with his humble manner.

Allen Iverson, the Philadelphia 76ers point guard who was Carter's teammate on the Eastern Conference team, told reporters after the game that he was most proud of a lob pass he threw to Carter during the game, because he wanted to be able to show his kids that he was an integral part of Carter's first All-Star appearance.

New York Knicks coach Jeff Van Gundy was more impressed by the way Carter handled himself off the court than he was by any of his acrobatics on it. Van Gundy was surprised when Carter went out of his way to apologize for being five minutes late for practice, and was equally surprised when Carter went to great lengths to introduce his parents to the man who'd coach him for just one All-Star game.

"He didn't have to do that. That tells you a lot about what kind of young man he is," Van Gundy said about Carter's off-court performance at the All-Star game.

Carter's kindness speaks volumes about his respect for his parents and those in positions of authority around him, and sets him apart from many other professional athletes. It is those personal qualities, as much as his skills as a player, that make Vince Carter stand out as an NBA superstar.

CHAPTER 1

In the Beginning

There wasn't really anything out of the ordinary about Vincent Lamar Carter in the first few years of his life. He was born on January 26, 1977, in Daytona Beach, Florida, into a middle-class family. He grew up surrounded by his mom, Michelle Carter-Robinson, his stepdad, Harry Robinson, and his younger brother, Christopher. He wasn't a particularly big baby, didn't come from an incredibly athletic family and, as he learned to walk and talk, there weren't any obvious signs of the greatness that would come to him later in life.

Yet there were tiny signals that something special was brewing inside. One of his cousins, Oliver Lee, had been an All-American basketball player at Marquette University in the 1950s; another distant cousin, who Carter didn't know at the time, was Tracy McGrady, who would eventually become Carter's Toronto Raptors teammate.

At the age of five, Vince recalls, he had already learned to dribble a basketball. "He was a baby-crib basketball player," says Dick Toth, the athletic director at Carter's high school, who was one of the first

JUST THE FACTS
Born: 1/26/77
Height: 6-6
Weight: 225

The future NBA superstar was born on January 26, 1977—
no one knew how great he would become when he grew up.

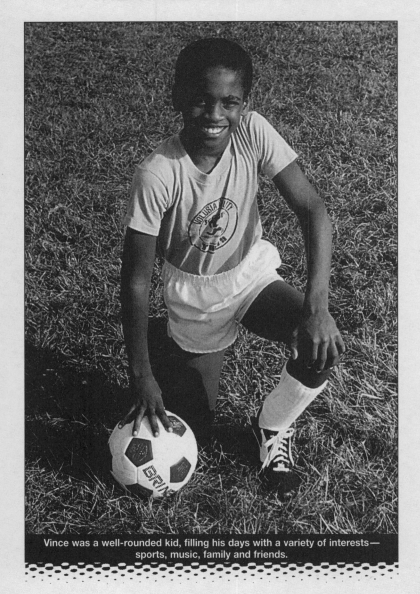

Vince was a well-rounded kid, filling his days with a variety of interests—
sports, music, family and friends.

men to coach him in the local YMCA basketball program. "At five years old, he could dribble without looking at the ball. He could put the ball between his legs and do crazy things. You could tell he was going to be a player."

But basketball wasn't the only thing Vince dedicated himself to in his preteen years. Although he had startling skills at a young age, he was just as interested in developing skills away from the playgrounds and the court. As early as fourth grade, Vince had developed an interest in computers and video games, hanging around after school at South Daytona Elementary School to play on the new computers the school had purchased. That started his lifelong passion for video games.

"I still play a lot," Vince admits. "I guess that got me hooked. At first, I just thought they were neat and a lot of kids my age started that young on them."

He also had a lot of opportunities to watch basketball on television as a kid, which led him to become a fan of one of the game's greatest players. It takes no thought for him to answer the popular question of who was his favorite player when he was growing up: "Dr. J. He was the best. I could watch him all day."

Of course, he's talking about Julius Erving, the legendary star of both the ABA and NBA who was, in his time, the most exciting player in the game. Erving had the kind

> # His favorite player when he was growing up? "Dr. J. He was the best. I could watch him all day."

On guard! Vince sits proudly as a grade school crossing guard.

of graceful moves that made it look as if he wasn't even working hard whenever he made one of his trademark dunks or simply laid the ball in the basket with the finger roll for which he's equally famous. That Vince should choose Erving as his favorite player comes as no surprise to people who watch Carter play today. The same characteristics that Erving displayed in his career also appear in the way Carter handles himself, both on and off the court.

Carter adopted one of Erving's most famous characteristics at a very young age. It has been said that Vince Carter did his first dunk as a 5-foot, 9-inch sixth grader on the gravel-tarmac court outside of Daytona's Ormond Middle School.

Carter claims that he doesn't really remember that first dunk, although his eyes do light up talking about it. "Ah," he says with a smile. "I don't remember it like it was yesterday. Just a little dunk. No one thought I could do it, but I guess I showed them."

CHAPTER 2

Family Ties

Carter's family background is different from many stories we hear about today's athletes. Carter's upbringing was, in many ways, the stuff of the 50s: full of family stability, discipline and a variety of interests. Vince's mom, Michelle, and Harry, his stepdad (whom Vince calls Dad), raised Vince and his younger brother, Christopher.

"I had a great upbringing," Vince once said in an interview. "I think that's had a lot to do with what I'm like today. My mom never let me get too big for myself, she kept me normal." His mom and dad laid down strict guidelines for his behavior: Never consider yourself better than anyone else, never hold your outstanding athletic ability over other people and, most important, treat others as you'd like to be treated.

There were family vacations and the typical big family gatherings at all holidays and birthday celebrations, which led to a close

> "I had a great upbringing. I think that's had a lot to do with what I'm like today. My mom never let me get too big for myself, she kept me normal."

While Vince was growing up, music was just as important to him as basketball.

> "My mom and dad made sure I did a little bit of everything. I think it helped me because I never got tired of doing one thing in particular."

family life and a happy childhood. "My parents were there to teach me, show me what was right and wrong and make sure I had the opportunities I needed," he said.

But basketball was never the number one activity around the Carter household as Vince was growing up. His mom was a teacher, and later a guidance counselor, at Mainland High School, and his stepdad taught at Mainland and was also the leader of the high school's marching band.

While the Carter house did have a basketball hoop outside—there was also a nearby park where Vince could go and get a game—the family made sure everyone had other interests as well. Schoolwork, music and time spent with family were just as important as basketball, baseball and football around their house.

"We just did all the normal things a family would do, I guess," Vince explained. "We'd have big birthday parties, get together for family events and just hang out. I think it was just normal. I never got pressured by anyone to play sports or do anything in particular.

"My mom and dad made sure I did a little bit of everything. I think it helped me because I never got tired of doing one thing in particular. I never got bored."

Before Vince led the Raptors to victory on the court, he was a drum major who led his school's marching band.

Balance has always been important in Vince's life—and his mom will always be there to make sure her oldest son realizes what he's doing and to make sure he never gets too big for himself.

Today, she is in charge of what those closest to Vince call Team Carter. Team Carter is the group of close friends, agents and advisers who help Vince deal with the demands that are

> "He may be Vince Carter to the world, but to me, he's my son and I'm going to do whatever I think is needed to make things best for him."

pulling him every which way every day. There are television commercial offers, requests for autograph sessions, media interviews—the requests to take a little bit of Vince's time are never-ending. He really counts on his group of trusted friends to help balance the requests and say no for him sometimes. And Vince's mom is the leader of this pack.

"He may be Vince Carter to the world, but to me, he's my son and I'm going to do whatever I think is needed to make things best for him," said his mother, who is a permanent fixture at Toronto Raptors games. "I'm always going to be there for him, to offer support and advice when he needs it. And I'm not going to let him get too big. When he comes home, he still has to put out the garbage."

Vince's family is still very close. During the first play-

Vince first represented the United States in the 1995 Junior World Championships.

> "What I said to Vince [before the summer began] was to just step back and think about what you can accomplish in one year... In one year, things people dream about their whole lives are happening for you."

off game in Raptors history, an Easter Sunday afternoon in New York's Madison Square Garden, Vince made sure that a member of the team's staff knew where his mom was sitting in the Garden. Just before the player introductions, the Raptors official stood on the Garden court and pointed to where Vince's mom was sitting, just so he'd know.

"It's one of the first things I do when she's at a game—find out where she is," Vince says. "I just want to know."

The closeness of the family goes far beyond knowing where his number one fan is sitting in any arena. His mother remains one of the steady influences in his life and is always someone who can put things in perspective for the young superstar. And thanks to his mom, while Vince was looking forward to playing in the 2000 Summer Olympics for the United States, he spent the summer finishing up his degree at the University of North Carolina.

Add those six weeks of summer school to a couple of kids' camps, a fantasy camp for adults, endorsement responsibilities and then the Olympics, and it's clear that Vince didn't have much downtime before training camp rolled around again right after the Games.

"What I said to Vince [before the summer began] was to just step back and think about what you can accomplish in one year, the first year of the millennium," Vince's mom said. "In one year, things people dream about their whole lives are happening for you. It sends chills down my spine."

CHAPTER 3

High School Superstar

Although Carter had been noticed as a young basketball star during his preteen years, it wasn't until he reached Mainland High School that he truly blossomed into a Florida schoolboy legend. But you could never tell what he had become by the way he acted.

The one thing most people remember about Carter as a high school student was his humility. Today, it's not unusual to hear about spectacular high school basketball players signing autographs in the hallway, strutting around as if they had already made it to the NBA. But Carter, taught well by his parents long before he got to high school, would never have presumed to be better than anyone else. He was just an ordinary high school kid who happened to have extraordinary athletic skills.

"Everybody loved Vince because he never got cocky," Dick Toth, Mainland's athletic director, told *The National Post* newspaper in Canada, years after those high school days. "Other kids shy away from those types of kids, the kids who get a little full of themselves when they get a little out of the ordinary. No one ever shied away from Vince. Everybody wanted to know where Vince was going to college; it was the guessing game of the day. With a lot of kids who get cocky, nobody cares what they do."

Vince Carter was a basketball legend loved by everyone at Mainland High School.

But they cared about Vince Carter very, very much. Carter's games at Mainland often had to be moved from the school's gym to the 6,100-seat Ocean Center in Daytona Beach, and every seat would be filled. When people couldn't get into the 700-seat high school gym for games, they would buy tickets and sit in the school's cafeteria to watch on closed circuit television. Although he wasn't cocky, Carter didn't mind the spotlight. In fact, he put on a real show by blocking 16 shots in a game on his 18th birthday—but he made sure to share the attention with his teammates.

> "High school basketball was great. It might have been the most fun I've ever had playing the game."

Joe Giddens, Carter's best friend and high school basketball teammate who became a standout football player at Bethune-Cookman College in Florida, remembers just what lengths Carter would go to in order to make sure he wasn't a one-man show. "He could have averaged something like fifty points a game and do whatever he wanted, whenever he wanted," Giddens said. "But he'd average like twenty points and keep everyone involved."

"High school basketball was great. It might have been the most fun I've ever had playing the game," Carter said. "Just playing with my buddies, the guys I grew up with, for my school, was special. It's something I'm always going to remember as a great time."

Although he led his Mainland team to the state cham-

Carter says that his days playing high school basketball were some of the most fun he has ever had: "Just playing with my buddies, the guys I grew up with, was special."

Carter led his high school team to the state championship in his senior year, while maintaining a wide variety of other interests as well.

pionship his senior year and was known as a high school basketball star, Carter's contribution to his school went far beyond his performance on the basketball court. He was involved in many other extracurricular activities. He was, and still is, a fine saxophone player and could be seen walking through the halls of Mainland toting his sax to music class as often as he was seen carrying his ball to basketball practice. In fact, his saxophone playing was so good that he was offered a music scholarship to Bethune-Cookman College, which he was very proud of but had to turn down because he knew his future was in basketball, not music.

> **"If there was one thing my mom and dad stressed all the time, it was the need to study and keep the grades up so I could play ball."**

He also served as the drum major in his high school band, which made his stepdad, the leader of his high school marching band, incredibly proud. Carter also wrote some poetry in his spare time, while carrying a B-average in his classes.

"I wasn't the greatest student, but I sure wasn't the worst, either," he recalls. "I knew I had to keep my grades up if I wanted to play basketball. If there was one thing my mom and dad stressed all the time, it was the need to study and keep the grades up so I could play ball."

His mom recalls being just as proud of her son's academic accomplishments in high school as his tremendous basketball talents. "Vince was a good student, he got good grades, he worked hard at academics, and that was important to us as a family," she said. "His hard work made us very, very proud."

Carter's basketball talents, though, were what caught the eye of people outside his circle of family and friends. In 1995, as an 18-year-old, he was selected to represent the United States at the world junior championships. Although the American team didn't win the gold medal, Carter's participation signaled his first major appearance on the national and international stage.

Away from the basketball court and band practice, Carter was very much the normal American teenager. He and his buddies would spend countless hours hanging out at the Volusia Mall in Daytona Beach, wasting away the after-school hours. Music, as one would guess, was a big part of the scene, and Carter could often be found patrolling the aisles of the mall's record store, trying to find something to add to his impressive CD collection. He liked a lot of different kinds of music, from rap to mellow jazz and blues.

"He'd have everything, it seemed," Giddens said about shopping for CDs with Vince. "We'd be look-

> "Vince was a good student, he got good grades, he worked hard at academics, and that was important to us as a family."

ing at the new releases and he'd be like, 'Got it, got it, got that one.' He'd ask what he was going to buy, but he'd always find something he didn't have."

Carter often attracted a crowd because of his basketball skills and local celebrity status. Many girls would gawk from a distance, but some were brave enough to come up to start a conversation. If Carter was being particularly shy or not acting the way his best friend Joe wanted, Giddens would march up to a bunch of teenagers, tell them who Carter was, then sit back and laugh as Carter tried to deal with the attention.

"Man, he'd get me all the time," recalls Vince. "I really didn't want to stand out, but sometimes Joe would make sure I did. It wasn't very comfortable."

Carter usually felt uncomfortable because he didn't want to create a scene. To this day, he is most happy just being one of the guys, no better and no worse than anybody else is. It was something hammered in at home. "So many kids come to school with baggage because they're so often from single-parent families and unstable homes; (Vince) had no baggage," said Charles Brinkerhoff, who coached Carter at Mainland. "He was just a good, normal, well-adjusted young man."

The thing most people wanted to know about Carter as his senior year of high school ended was where he was going to go to college. As the best high school basketball player in the state, there were no shortages of scholarship offers. Carter figures he had almost 80 serious offers to choose from, and the decision was not an easy one to make. He wanted to go to a school where basketball was the most popular sport. He also wanted to go somewhere

Carter was widely recognized as a great basketball player throughout high school—he received scholarship offers from more than 80 colleges.

where he'd be academically challenged. He wanted to stay close to home, where his mom, dad, brother and friends could see him play without too much time or traveling.

It took some time and a lot of thought for him to reach a decision. When it came time to make the announcement that everyone was waiting for, his decision didn't come as much of a surprise.

He had chosen North Carolina, the home of the legendary Tar Heels.

CHAPTER 4

Tar Heels, Here He Comes!

There are few college basketball programs that have the rich traditions that exist at the University of North Carolina. The team is always a contender for the national championship and has fans in every corner of the continent. The players who make the team are under intense scrutiny from the time they commit as high schoolers to the time they leave college. It takes a special type of player to survive and do well at North Carolina.

Under the legendary Tar Heels coach Dean Smith, seniors are usually the focus of the team, both on and off the court; they get the majority of shots each game and are to be treated with respect by the underclassmen.

It was into this atmosphere that 18-year-old Vince Carter arrived, and there were times when he wondered if he'd made the right decision. As a freshman, under Smith's rule, Carter spent more time on the bench than he ever had in his life, sitting and watching other players who were not as good as Carter thought that he could be.

"I never really regretted my decision, but I think maybe I thought too much of myself coming out of high school. At some level maybe I was a bit full of myself," he said. "It was tough, I was sitting and I was-

Vince went to college at the University of North Carolina to play for the legendary Tar Heels, following in the footsteps of one of the greatest players of all time—Michael Jordan.

n't used to that....I was sort of doubting myself because I really didn't know what was going on."

Neither did Carter's parents or his fans back in Daytona. His mom even joked that the whole city of Daytona thought about driving to Chapel Hill to confront Coach Smith and demand that he explain why Vince was on the bench.

> "I was never into that stuff. Sure, I had fun, I was in college, but I never went overboard. I had a lot of stuff to take care of— classes and basketball."

In that freshman year, Carter did appear in all but one of North Carolina's games, but he didn't get to play extended minutes and averaged only 7.5 points and 3.8 rebounds a game, which was a huge letdown from his high school performances.

Away from the court, Carter lived like any other Tar Heel basketball player, on the sixth floor of West Granville Towers, a dormitory complex that had for years been the home of North Carolina hoopsters. While some might think the dorm life would lead to plenty of parties, Carter never took part. To this day, he has never had a drink and never smoked. When friends from home would visit, he'd take them out to the Chapel Hill nightspots, but he always resisted the invitations of free drinks from bartenders and other people who wanted to be his pal.

"I was never into that stuff," he recalls. "Sure, I had

fun, I was in college, but I never went overboard. I had a lot of stuff to take care of—classes and basketball—and there wasn't any time for that other stuff."

Although Vince didn't play much his first year, Smith was more than happy to let players blossom in their sophomore, junior and senior seasons and to start taking on a bigger role in the team's system.

Carter, of course, shined when given the chance. After his disappointing freshman season, he returned for his second year and was immediately more confident in his role and more relied upon by Smith. There were glimpses of the great player he would become. He averaged 13.0 points and 4.5 rebounds and was chosen to the NCAA's All-East Regional team. He also helped the Tar Heels make it to the Final Four, where they were beaten in the semifinals by the Arizona Wildcats. Carter says the accomplishment of getting to the Final Four remains one of his proudest moments as an athlete, and capped off a breakthrough season for the soon-to-be star.

"You could tell by the look on his face that he was having fun," his mom said about Vince's sophomore season. "The spring was back in his step. We all relaxed a little when we saw that, because we knew he was going to be okay."

Things were going great off the court, as well. Carter was one of the most popular players on the team and was equally comfortable with the students in his classes. His reputation was that of a respectful young man who had his priorities straight.

As his junior year unfolded, Carter was becoming more and more successful. The basketball skills he had

Vince worked hard to fit into Coach Dean Smith's system at North Carolina.

FOOT FANCY

It's a little known fact that very few NBA players are proud of their feet. Years and years of stops and starts in practices and games on hard floors takes its toll on feet. Carter is no different. When friends would stop by his dorm room in college, an often-barefoot Carter would stick his feet into pillowcases to hide them.

shown as a high school standout were on display as he became an integral part of the North Carolina team. Although he still played in the shadow of his teammate and good friend Antawn Jamison, Vince showed even more flashes of the skills that would soon make him an NBA All-Star. He finished the season averaging 15.6 points, 5.1 rebounds and 1.9 assists. He was named a finalist for the prestigious John R. Wooden Award for college player of the year, was a second-team All-American and was a First Team All-Atlantic Coast Conference selection.

"I knew he was the best player in college basketball since my freshman season," said Ed Cota, the point guard who threw Carter all kinds of alley-oop passes for two years. "But when you play in a program like North Carolina, everybody takes a role. So you're not going to be able to show everything you can do out there. But you're going to get a glimpse of it. And that's what people overlooked. They saw little glimpses and then they forgot about it."

But the NBA scouts were very aware of Carter's abilities, and many saw in him the makings of an exceptional pro player, although they were not sure how great he would become. "Scouting North Carolina was always tricky because of Coach Dean Smith's strict system," said Bob Zuffelato, the Toronto Raptors director of basket-ball operations who spent countless days watching Carter play in college. "I won't say his kids are held back, but he emphasized teamwork and fundamentals at the expense of individualism. A lot of people were even fooled on Michael Jordan when he was there."

> **"A kid like Vince was suppressed in a way, but a better all-around player when he came out."**

Adds Raptors general manager Glen Grunwald: "You had to evaluate these people in the context of how Smith did things. A kid like Vince was suppressed in a way, but a better all-around player when he came out. But the flair he has as a pro was difficult to spot."

After his junior year, Carter and his family knew they had to explore the possibility that he would be one of the top picks in the upcoming NBA Draft. Unwilling to just go by the word of those closest to them, the family sought the advice of ex-NBA players, current coaches and players and scouts before making what was to be one of the biggest decisions of Vince's life.

It was only after plenty of investigation and soul-searching that the decision was reached. It was time to take the next step: It was time to leap into the NBA.

As a basketball decision, it turned out to be a no-brainer. Carter had accomplished everything except winning a national title during his three years at North Carolina. He had shown incredible ability but had reached his college peak. He wasn't going to get better playing a senior season in the NCAA, and the next logical challenge was the NBA.

And both he and his family knew the education he had gotten in his three years at North Carolina wasn't going to be wasted. Carter was ready for the NBA, of that there was no doubt. He would be back to finish school several years later to make good on an educational promise he made to his family before he started college. But first, it was time to play ball.

CHAPTER 5

Rookie of the Year

The NBA Draft is not something that teams take lightly. They must reward each first-round pick with a three-year guaranteed contract, but that's not the most important part of the draft for most organizations. Most teams, especially those clubs that didn't make it as far as the playoffs the previous season, often look to their first-round draft picks to revitalize the team and lead it to the playoffs.

That's why teams go to such great lengths to investigate the players they are considering as first-round selections. They watch dozens and dozens of college games, hold individual workouts for specific players and do background checks to find out what kind of family situation the players came from.

They hope to find a perfect fit, the perfect marriage between a team's needs and a player's skills.

Toronto Raptors? Meet Vince Carter.

The day of the 1998 NBA Draft arrived with a lot of questions in people's minds. The Los Angeles Clippers, who had the first pick, were still deciding whether to choose center Michael Olowokandi or guard Mike Bibby; the Vancouver Grizzlies liked and needed Bibby but were not sure if he'd still be available after the Clippers had selected. The Denver Nuggets, who had the third choice,

The Toronto Raptors knew, without a doubt, which player they wanted in the 1998 NBA Draft: Vince Carter, the future Schick NBA Rookie of the Year.

were really interested in center Raef LaFrentz but would have taken Olowokandi had both the Clippers and the Grizzlies passed him up.

Picking fourth, the Toronto Raptors knew their selection would be determined largely by what went on before them in the picking order. But they knew without a doubt which player they wanted: Vince Carter.

> **"I really didn't know what was going on. I was just happy to get drafted into the NBA."**

"He had been so good in the workout it was a no-brainer," said then-Raptors coach Butch Carter. "We just had to wait and make sure we could get him. We knew it was going to be a huge day for the franchise if we pulled it off."

But they had no problem pulling it off. They had bluffed the Golden State Warriors, who had the fifth pick, into thinking they were interested in Antawn Jamison, the NCAA player of the year, and Carter's more notorious North Carolina teammate. They let it be known, however, that they'd trade Jamison to any other team that wanted him.

The Warriors, it turned out, wanted him very badly. Toronto, in a move agreed to on draft afternoon, picked Jamison, planning to trade him to Golden State for Carter, who would be chosen one selection later. That way, both teams would get what they wanted, and the Warriors didn't have to worry about the Raptors taking Jamison and trading him to some other team.

At the draft, both Carter and Jamison were taken

aback by the quick trade. They didn't know about the deal that had been made earlier in the day.

"I really didn't know what was going on, I was just happy to get drafted into the NBA," Carter said. "Toronto had treated me well during my visit there, so it was okay with me."

Carter's NBA debut was delayed nearly four months by the NBA lockout, but once the day finally arrived, he never had time to look back. His first game ever was in Boston's FleetCenter, and he scored 16 points as the Raptors upset the Celtics to begin what would turn into the best season in club history.

Showing off an array of spectacular dunks, Carter quickly established himself as one of the league's most exciting young players. But in typical fashion, he downplayed his accomplishments by saying that he was just taking advantage of the opportunities that presented themselves and just trying to help his team win. Privately, teammates and Raptors officials were amazed by his athletic ability and all-around skills. "We knew Vince was going to be good; we didn't know he was

PHONE PALS

NBA teammates spend an awful lot of time with one another, so you might think they'd like to get away from one another from time to time. Wrong. Sometimes during his rookie season, Vince would pull out his cell phone and dial up one of his closest friends. About a dozen seats away, Tracy McGrady would hear his phone ring, pick it up and start a conversation—with Vince.

Vince amazed Toronto fans with his awesome sky-high dunks during his first year in the NBA.

going to be that good, that fast," said General Manager Glen Grunwald, who was praised by rival teams for recognizing Carter's potential in the first place.

In that rookie season, Carter also displayed the flair for the dramatic that would become a hallmark of his talents in his sophomore season. On the day the Raptors christened their brand-new arena, a 19,800-seat palace called the Air Canada Centre, Carter exploded for 27 points, six rebounds, five assists and six steals in a win over the NBA's other

> "We knew Vince was going to be good; we didn't know he was going to be that good."

Canadian club, the Vancouver Grizzlies. That performance cemented his reputation as a big-game player, which is something he's proud of but never brings up himself.

"We were just starting to see how good Vince really was," recalls his coach at the time, Butch Carter. "The really great players can sense a moment. Vince can do that."

In leading Toronto to its best winning percentage ever, Carter continued to startle the fans who were seeing him for the first time. In 23 of Toronto's 50 games, he led the team in scoring. He finished the season averaging 18.3 points per game, the best record on the team, as well as 5.7 rebounds and 3.0 assists.

Because of Carter's tremendous skill, a Toronto team that had won only 16 of 82 games the year before was actually in the running for an Eastern Conference playoff berth, which they lost in the last two weeks of the regular season. By that time, though, Carter had earned the respect of everyone he played with and against, and the fans had all come to love him.

"He's not like a lot of the kids, not too much into himself," said Charles Oakley, a 15-year NBA veteran who arrived with Carter in

> # "He's about the team, not too much hype. Some kids, it's all hype. He knows how to play."

Toronto for the 1999 season. "He's about the team, not too much hype. Some kids, it's all hype. He knows how to play."

As he became more comfortable as an NBA player and a budding star, he became more outspoken about his desire to lead his team up the standings. As the Raptors became embroiled in their playoff race his rookie year, he spoke loudly and often about doing whatever it took to win and earn the first playoff berth in franchise history. For Toronto fans, unaccustomed to such success, the words provided a lot of hope for the team's future, hope that had never before existed. Because of Carter's words, the fans hoped for greater times to come.

Carter's role as the public spokesman for the team was most obvious after the last game of the regular season, when the playoffs were no longer a possibility but when the future shone brighter than it ever had before. Grabbing the microphone after an end-of-the-season ceremony at the Air Canada Centre, Carter promised the sold-out stadium that the next season would bring a playoff berth. He was setting himself up to disappoint his fans if he didn't make good on his word, but it was a risk he was willing to take.

"I didn't really think about it. I just said it because I believed it," he said later.

There was just one little thing to take care of in the days after that impromptu speech that buoyed the spirits of the team's fans. It was really just a formality, but it was one that perfectly capped Carter's dramatic NBA debut.

There are 118 members of the North American media who vote for the NBA's awards, and it had become apparent early in the season that Carter was the odds-on favorite to be named the Schick NBA Rookie of the Year. While many of those voters had not seen him perform in person often, they had all seen him during games against Toronto and were well aware of his skills.

When the votes had been cast, the result was astounding. Carter had received 113 of 118 votes, the third most in NBA history, behind only Shaquille O'Neal(1993) and Tim Duncan(1998). Winning this award established Carter as the dominant player of his class, and it also made it clear that Toronto would get great things out of him in the future. But more than anything, it made Toronto a team other NBA players wanted to play for.

Knowing that, Carter said, "I have to set a standard around here and tell people that if you want to come and play for the Toronto Raptors, you have to be dedicated to this organization, you have to be dedicated to hard work, and you have to be ready to play every night."

Of all the tremendous things Carter did in his rookie season for himself and for the Raptors, that statement had the biggest impact in turning the franchise around.

CHAPTER 6

Vinsanity, Year 2

One of the most difficult things Vince Carter has ever had to do is live up to his own reputation. An 82-game NBA schedule can be grueling at times, with three or four games a week and difficult travel that make the bumps and bruises a player picks up hurt just a little bit more.

Throw into that equation the hype that kicked into overdrive in Carter's second season, and living up to the reputation he had earned in his rookie season was hard to do. After all, Carter had been the most electrifying rookie to come into the game in years, and as he started his second season, everyone wanted more. Including, of course, success-starved Toronto Raptors fans, who expected him to live up to his guarantee of getting the team to the playoffs for the first time.

So it was against this backdrop that Carter began his sophomore season. And, as always, he didn't disappoint.

One trait Carter showed regularly throughout his second season was being able to rise to the occasion when the lights were the brightest. In their five-year history, the Raptors had not been much more than a curiosity to many NBA fans, but that had all changed, thanks primarily to Carter. NBC, the network that airs NBA games, had never shown a Raptors game, caught wind of Carter's abilities at the All-Star Game and NBA.com Slam Dunk

Carter had been the most electrifying rookie to come into the game in years, and as he started his second season, everyone wanted more.

and decided to televise a Raptors-Phoenix Suns game from Air Canada Centre.

"It's about time," Carter joked about having a Raptors game televised. "I guess before they never thought it was worth showing a Raptors game. It says a lot about how far the team has come. Maybe if they show one, they'll come back for more and we'll be on national TV all the time."

Not only did the Raptors win the game, 103–102, as a sold-out crowd went crazy, but Carter exploded for 51 points, which was, at that point, the single-biggest offensive output by an NBA player that season. He hit three-pointers and dunks, made layups and midrange jump shots and startled the national television audience with his wide range of abilities.

"And the legend grows," marveled Butch Carter after that game.

The raves continued throughout the entire season. Carter finished the season fourth in the league in scoring, averaging 25.7 points and topping 30 points 25 times. He was also his team's most accurate three-point shooter (.403), which proved he was committed to working on all aspects of his game instead of just settling for his explosive dunking abilities.

He became one of the most popular players in the game, leading the voting for a spot on the All-Star team — he had received 1,911,973, the second-highest total ever recorded. Of course, he won the NBA.com Slam Dunk, with an incredible move nobody had ever seen before.

He was twice voted the NBA's Player of the Week and led the league in scoring in the months of December and

February. He went on to lead Toronto in scoring, field goal percentage and three-point percentage, while coming in second in assists, third in blocked shots and steals and fifth in rebounds. Not bad for a guy who at one time had a reputation as being only a dunker.

> "He's probably the most exciting individual in basketball right now. Basically, he's a human-highlight film."

"He's probably the most exciting individual in basketball right now," Cavaliers power forward Shawn Kemp said. "Basically, he's a human-highlight film."

The first time he played the Lakers in Los Angeles, fans were in their seats before game time to check out his dunks in the layup lines. "Half man, half amazing," declared Shaquille O'Neal after the game.

"People say give him the jump shot, which is ludicrous," Knicks coach Jeff Van Gundy has said about Carter. "He's got the ability to post, he has the intermediate game, he can get to the rim and he can get to the line, and last year against us hit two late threes to seal the deal (in a Toronto win).

"So, offensively he has the whole deal. Those are the guys most difficult to deal with in our league. One-dimensional players—drivers or shooters—those guys you can handle. It's guys who have short, long and intermediate games that give you problems."

With three spots left to fill on the American Olympic

team for the 2000 Sydney Games, it was thought that Carter would get one of the slots when the names were announced in early January. But he was not chosen by the selection committee. Carter was upset when it looked as if he'd be unable to fulfill one of his biggest goals in life—representing his country in the Olympics.

So when the Raptors faced U.S. Olympic Team member Ray Allen and the Bucks a couple of nights later, Carter went off for 47 points in a 115–110 Toronto victory. He played with a ferocity that night that had seldom been seen, and showed that deep down he was a fierce competitor who, when challenged, would answer with force.

Eventually, people took notice. So when Tom Gugliotta of the Phoenix Suns went down with a season-ending injury about a month after the team had been selected and had to give up his spot on the Olympic team, a call quickly went out to Carter.

He was added to the team for the Sydney Games in a moment he calls "one of the best things that's happened to me in basketball. It's a great honor to represent your country."

All his varied skills created an incredible buzz around Carter. It was as if he were a rock star. One night in Dallas, he had four incredible dunks, one of which came at the end of a fast break when he exploded from the free-throw line, took a pass while in the air and finished with a startling dunk. The next time a whistle went to stop play, Mavericks fans in the arena looked quickly to the video board to see the dunk again. When a replay of a Mavericks player being fouled was shown instead, the

The "half man, half amazing" Carter wowed everyone in the NBA in his second season.

fans booed long and loud. That was the kind of impact that Carter had—even in hostile, out-of-town environments.

"It's like the Beatles. Incredible," one teammate said after security guards were needed to help escort Carter from the STAPLES Center in Los Angeles after he had won yet another game at the buzzer, this time with a three-pointer from far beyond the arc.

It was indeed Vinsanity.

At one point in the season, Carter said he wished he could just visit cities, meet up with old pals and just hang around with them in a mall or a club. That was simply not possible.

"Life's not real easy right now but I guess I'd rather have it this way than not at all," he said.

But through his rising fame, Carter didn't really change. He had the same "team-first" attitude he had shown in his magical rookie season and throughout high school and college. He remained committed to the success of his team—he'd make sure to hit open teammates with passes instead of forcing shots and trying to create something that wasn't there, and no one ever got the impression he thought he was bigger or more important than the team or the game. He is completely unselfish, and that just further endears him to teammates and those who truly appreciate the game of basketball.

Although Vince's sophomore season would eventually end in disappointment—Toronto was knocked out of its first playoff series in three straight games by the Knicks—Vinsanity had reached an incredible level. At just 23 years old, and after just two seasons in the NBA, Vince was being compared with the greats of all time. "I can't really think about that stuff," he said of that comparison. "It's an honor and everything, but I don't listen a lot to what people say. I just go out and play and we'll see what happens."

New York coach Jeff Van Gundy, who has seen many good players in his day, suggested the only thing that could stop Carter was Carter himself. "If he's driven, he'll be one of the greats in this league for a long time, and perhaps one of the greatest of all time," he said.

CHAPTER 7

Back to School

It was a gorgeous late spring afternoon on the pretty, tree-lined campus of the University of North Carolina in Chapel Hill. The meeting place bounded by the student union, a bookstore, a dining hall and the undergraduate library were all bustling with activity.

In the middle of it all, completely anonymous to the hundreds who parade across campus, there was a guy who looked like any other typical student. He had the dress—sunglasses, shorts, T-shirt, sneakers and a cap worn backward; and he had the books, backpack and homework assignments.

But he was far from the typical college student picking up a couple of extra credits in the first summer semester. It was Vince Carter, NBA All-Star, sports hero to millions and one of the last guys one would expect to be filling five hours a day with biology classes and labs.

The 23-year-old superstar, just like other students, was taking a break from classes and labs that kept him busy for eight weeks as he pursued a degree in African-American studies during the summer of 2000.

"I come here because it's quiet, I feel comfortable

Superstar slam dunker at night, student by day—Vince Carter does it all.

here, and it's a bonus that you can just come to school and be yourself," he said. "I'm just like any other North Carolina student and it's fun."

The fact that he spent a good chunk of his offseason studying speaks volumes about the well-rounded nature of Carter's personality and his commitment to finishing something that he started.

Carter completed his degree to honor a promise he made to his mom. When he first accepted a scholarship to North Carolina, he signed a contract with his mom promising that he'd get his degree.

After three years as a Tar Heel, Carter's basketball abilities had become too great for the college game, and if he was going to continue to be challenged athletically, it would have to be at the professional level. But he knew that after he left college there would have to be other things in his life besides basketball.

That's one thing that his mom always wanted, too. For an offseason that's always crammed with camps, endorsement obligations and, in 2000 at least, the Olympics, Michelle Carter-Robinson feels her son needs to take time to just live a little.

"These kids all want to be adults and get out into the

VINCE FACTS AND FUN
Favorite Food: Chicken
Favorite Movie: *Coming to America*
Favorite Basketball Player: Julius "Dr. J" Erving
Hobbies: Playing the saxophone, watching television, Sega

real world so fast, sometimes that's not all it's cracked up to be," she said. "I think Vince should just go back to class and be a regular kid; there will be all the time in the world for the rest of that stuff."

Carter didn't return to school just to keep the promise he had made to his mom. He found he

> "I'm here for me. I promised my mom I'd do it, but now it's something I want to do. I'm excited about it."

actually liked the idea of getting his college degree. He spent the offseason between his rookie and second NBA seasons taking classes, and after the summer of 2000, he finally had enough credits to graduate. He knew he would feel a huge sense of accomplishment putting on the cap and gown for the graduation ceremony.

"I'm here for me," he said after he went back to school. "I promised my mom I'd do it, but now it's something I want to do. I'm excited about it."

Going back to school also gave him a chance to be a regular guy, and Carter appreciated the privacy.

"I think I've only signed two autographs since I got here," he said while at North Carolina for summer classes. "I think people think, hey, I'm here trying to graduate and I think maybe they see it as a positive thing. A couple people in class were telling me to keep studying, giving me an idea of what the class was like. It's nice to be a little bit normal."

Trying to be normal was one big reason Carter decided

to take summer classes. He gets enough of the royal treatment every day of the NBA season and went back to school when there would be fewer students on campus.

"The first day, everyone was, like, 'There's Vince, there's Vince,'" said Joe Giddens, who is still Carter's best friend and joined Vince at UNC to give his buddy a close friend to hang around with. "I think even the teacher was excited. But we just sat in the back and no one bothered us."

Carter also decided to go back to school so he could provide a true, firsthand message when he talks to teenagers. In the speeches he gives at public appearances during the basketball season, Carter likes to point out the need for a good education, and now his audience can see that he practices what he preaches.

> "I talk to a lot of kids and that's one message I'm most proud of. I can tell them how important school is, and then they see me going back to get my degree."

"I talk to a lot of kids and that's one message I'm most proud of," he said. "I can tell them how important school is, and then they see me going back to get my degree. For me to do it is important. In middle school or in high school, you don't think about school too much, or a degree. This is a way of showing them how important it is to me. And when I'm done playing bas-

Vince went back to school between his rookie and sophomore seasons so that he could experience being a "regular guy" again.

"You might see anything in those classes. I'm seeing a lot of things I never thought I would."

ketball, I'll have a degree maybe I can use." Although he doesn't intend to give up basketball for a teaching career or anything else, he said the most important aspect of getting his degree was the sense of accomplishment it brought.

Although he was a busy student, Carter always found time to get into the gym a couple of nights each week to scrimmage with the members of the university's team who stuck around for summer school, along with the other NBA players who would drop by.

But more than anything, classes provide an interesting change from his usual NBA life. For example, in one of his courses he had a biology lab that studied insects and butterflies, then a couple of weeks later he took part in the dissection of a pig. Those are not things many NBA players are familiar with. "You might see anything in those classes," he said. "I'm seeing a lot of things I never thought I would."

CHAPTER 8

The Future Calls

So where does Vince Carter go from here? How good can he become? How much more popular can he get? As Knicks coach Jeff Van Gundy said, Carter has the chance to be one of the best players in the long history of the NBA if he dedicates himself to continued improvement. But it's not as if Carter needs someone to tell him that. He knows better than anyone that nothing good comes from resting on past success. If you don't get better, you get left behind. And there's always someone on the horizon to challenge you.

"I'm always working to improve. I know there are parts of my game that can get better and that's what I work on," he says. "Nobody ever won a championship by settling, and I'm not going to."

There are two very specific instances that show just how dedicated Carter is to improving and developing his total game. Before his rookie season, the Toronto coaching staff suggested he might want to work to improve his left-hand dribble, so he wouldn't get to be known as a player who could only go one way on the court, something opponents would quickly pick up on and would seriously limit his game. He went back to North Carolina and Daytona that summer, spent hours in the gym alone, and showed up for his first camp using both hands equally well.

So what does the future hold for Vince? "You play to be a champion; that's what it's all about," he says.

After his stellar rookie season, he feared becoming known as a one-dimensional player, someone who could get to the rim and finish with ferocity, but someone who couldn't win games from outside the lane. Again, he spent a huge chunk of his summer in the gym, shooting hundreds and hundreds of jump shots a day, until he became one of the best young shooters in the NBA. The results were startling: He went from shooting 28.8 percent from three-point range in his rookie season to shooting 40.3 percent in his second season, a dramatic improvement some thought impossible. It added a dimension to his game that made him virtually unstoppable.

> "He's not going to be satisfied with himself until he's a complete player....When we give him something to work on, he does it."

"It shows you the dedication he has," Vince's first NBA coach, Butch Carter, once said. "He's not going to be satisfied with himself until he's a complete player. A lot of young players think they can just get by on their talent, they don't realize how much work has to be done to improve. When we give him something to work on, he does it."

But Carter knows the true measure of greatness is winning. He realizes that the superstars who have gone before him have one thing he doesn't yet—an NBA championship, or at the very least an appearance in the NBA Finals.

"Getting a ring, that's what it's all about," he said. "You play to be a champion, that's what drives me all the time. I need to make myself better, I need to make my teammates better, and we need to just keep getting better every year."

After guiding Toronto to its first-ever playoff appearance, Carter was left stung by the team's postseason performance against the New York Knicks. He realized that although great things can happen in a regular season, when that same level of intensity isn't enough for the postseason, there is still work to be done.

"People can tell you about [the playoffs] all they want, veterans and guys who have been there, but until you experience it yourself, you really don't know what it's like," Carter said after the Raptors' 2000 playoffs ended. "I'll know better next time what I have to do."

Carter also knows that in order to truly succeed, his impact must be felt away from the basketball court as well. Carter continues to make his mark outside of basketball through charitable organizations. His Embassy of Hope Foundation helps with mentoring programs for elementary and middle school students. His annual celebrity softball game and golf tournament raises thousands of dollars each summer for his foundation, which then returns the money to communities.

He has also established Vince's Hoop Group, which recognizes students of achievement at various local high schools and rewards them with tickets to Raptors games and a chance to meet their hero.

"It's important to be involved in the community," he says. "I like being able to help students. Maybe they can see that with hard work and dedication they can accomplish their goals like I did. Maybe they won't be basketball players, but they can see that if they put their minds to it, they can become teachers, business leaders, whatever they want to do."

> "I like being able to help students. Maybe they can see that with hard work and dedication they can accomplish their goals like I did."

There has been nothing in his past that would suggest Carter will settle for anything less than excellence in whatever he does. He's already one of the most well-liked players in the NBA, on and off the court, and he continues to create his own reputation.

One thing that upsets Carter more than anything are the comparisons between him and the legendary Michael Jordan, which began during Carter's rookie season and have continued since then.

Sure, they both played at North Carolina, both broke onto the NBA scene as high-flying dunkers, and each was asked to turn around the fortunes of a team that had been struggling. Jordan, of course, went on to be considered by many as the greatest man to ever play the game, and Carter has yet to win a playoff series.

As Carter has quickly pointed out from his first day in the league, Jordan was Jordan, Carter is Carter, and the

After only two seasons in the league, Carter was already being compared to the legendary Michael Jordan.

FOR THE RECORD

High School: Mainland High School
(Daytona Beach, Florida)
College: University of North Carolina
Major in College: African-American Studies
Drafted: 5th overall (1998)
Most Points Per Game: 51 (vs. Phoenix, 2/27/00)
Most Rebounds Per Game: 15 (vs. New Jersey, 3/16/99)
Most Assists Per Game: 10 (vs. Cleveland, 4/10/00)

young phenom just wants to carve his own place in the game. "I am who I am," he said. "There's a lot of pressure being the next 'man.' I'm my own person, and I want to establish my own identity. And everybody in the NBA has flashes of playing like Mike sometime. I'm just honored by the comparison but I want to be me.

"I'm really just trying to stay away from it. I'm trying to find my own identity."

His identity has become established in the two seasons Carter has already spent in the NBA. He has become known as someone who respects the game and respects his teammates, coaches and opponents. He is someone who accepts the huge responsibility that has been placed on him—the responsibility to make his team better and the responsibility that comes with being a role model for millions of young people who want to be like Vince Carter.

In his time in the league, he has handled himself with dignity and class, making his team better, making himself better and making his fans see that through hard work and commitment, goals can be achieved.

The future shines bright for the young superstar.

From his exceptional family upbringing, where becoming a well-rounded individual was more important than athletic achievements, to his first two years in the NBA, Carter has become a man to be respected. There is no suggestion that he won't continue to command that respect as his career progresses.

> # "I'm looking forward to the future. I'm just having a lot of fun and I don't think that's going to change."

"I'm looking forward to the future," he said. "I'm just having a lot of fun and I don't think that's going to change."

Vinsanity has only just begun....Look out, world, here comes Vince!

CAREER HiGHLiGHTS

★ As a 5-9 sixth grader, young Vince throws down his first dunk at a playground in Daytona Beach.

★ As a senior, leads Mainland High School to state basketball championship.

★ As a North Carolina sophomore, leads Tar Heels to NCAA Final Four. Finishes three-year college career averaging 12.3 points, 4.5 rebounds and 1.9 assists in 103 career games.

★ Is named second-team All-American after UNC junior year, when he was also a finalist for the John R. Wooden Award for the NCAA's best player; also named to First-Team All-Atlantic Coast Conference All-Star team.

★ Selected fifth overall in 1998 NBA Draft by Golden State Warriors but is immediately dealt from Warriors to Toronto Raptors for college teammate Antawn Jamison in a prearranged trade.

★ As an NBA rookie, becomes first Raptor ever named NBA Player of the Week for March 21, 1999, and is also selected NBA Rookie of the Month in March.

★ Landslide winner of NBA Schick Rookie of the Year Award, winning 113 of 118 votes. Finishes rookie

CAREER HiGHLiGHTS

season averaging **18.3 points, 5.7 rebounds,** and is a unanimous selection to All-Rookie team.

★ Leading vote-getter in fan voting for 1999–2000 NBA All-Star game—he receives **1,911,973 votes,** the second-highest total in history and best ever for a Raptor. Scores **12 points** and gets four rebounds in the game.

★ Wins NBA.com 2000 Slam Dunk as part of All-Star Weekend festivities, scoring perfect marks on three of his dunks.

★ Named NBA Player of the Week twice (November 15–21 and February 21–27).

★ Leads entire NBA in scoring for December 1999 (27.4 points per game) and February 2000 (29.8 points per game).

★ Scores 30 or more points in 25 of Toronto's 82 games in 1999–2000, including career-high 51 points in a 103-102 win over Phoenix.

★ Leads Raptors to first playoff berth in franchise history as they finish sixth in the NBA's Eastern Conference.

★ Named third-team All-NBA.

An All-Star Lineup of NBA Action That Can't Be Beat!

where the women grasped every opportunity to fling themselves into each other's arms the moment the men went hunting or rushed out on the war path. The well-known Indian smoke-signals are really vaginal symbols sent up by lesbian squaws. But no culture can be compared with that of the Eskimos. Here women warmed their bodies reciprocally in the igloos while their men were out fishing in holes in the ice (and hours could pass between each bite).

The fact that Xanthippe was a lesbian is clear from the fact that Plato carefully avoids mentioning it. About men's love for each other he wasn't so reticent, but that's something else, of course. This proves that the Athenian woman, on the whole, had sexual intercourse with her female servants, while her husband unknowingly made democracy on the Acropolis. Not to mention the oracle at Delphi.

About lesbian joy in the Inca kingdom little is known, because there are no written reports. But some anthropological research has just started, based on the hypothesis that quipu writing can be interpreted as breast fixation, and the explanation is sought in certain lesbian orgies that took place in the Andes mountains at the solstice. Especially around Lake Titicaca.

I presume that these theories were totally unknown to you. I can only recommend you to start reading all the extensive scientific writings on the subject. And then you'll see that when one finally realises that one is a lesbian, one feels that one is the bearer of great cultural traditions.

THREE

Thus was my life

Gunnhild and I agreed that since we were now going to make our entrance into the world of lesbians, we should no longer be lovers. Our loneliness would cease and, besides, how were we to get a chance with other women if everyone thought we were together?

The day finally arrived. We went to the Central Railway Station, and just in front of us walked a girl with short fair hair and rapid determined steps. 'I'm sure she is going *there*,' said Gunnhild. 'Oh, don't be a fool,' I said. She didn't look like a lesbian in the least. When we found the right train, the girl sat in our compartment. And when we got off at our station, the girl got off, too, and disappeared with her rapid determined steps into the darkness.

Now 'I.Hansen' turned up and greeted us – it was one of the secretaries from the Tuesday – and we went through the fog, down an alley and a path towards the fjord. It was a damp November night and the Society of 1948 seemed to have their meetings at a rowing club. 'I.Hansen' knocked at the door. Someone opened it a crack, just wide enough for a nose and a keen eye to peep through. 'Here I am with the two new ones!' Now the door was opened wide, and 'I.Hansen' said to a rather handsome man in a red waistcoat, black trousers and a tie, 'Will you please look after the two ladies, Helen?' Yes. 'Helen' promised to escort us into the dancing room and find us a place. There, in a corner, the girl from the train was sitting alone at a table. We went up to her and asked her if we could join her.

I shall never forget how shocked I was the first time I went to the Norwegian Society of 1948. First, I was deeply shocked because people looked just about as ordinary as people on Carl Johan Street in the rush hour. Secondly, I was shocked to see two men dancing together. It looked extremely peculiar. The roots of my hair prickled as I watched. They downright clung to each other and gazed into each other's eyes and so on.

I stared at them fascinated, although my mum had told me not to stare at peculiar people. (In my home town I used to walk backwards after having passed them.) I wasn't all that shocked to see the girls. Of course, I wasn't completely unshocked either. But it's different with girls, don't you think?

But now I'm not being quite honest. There were certain ladies there who corresponded completely to the kind of notion one has of a lesbian woman when one is prejudiced – like you are – and hasn't got a clue. You know, the kind of lady in a male suit who looks so masculine, especially from behind, that one knows it can't possibly be a man? Believe me, the 'Helen' that we had met at the door wasn't a 'Helen' in inverted commas at all. She was a lady. You already guessed that? Well, I want you to know that I was deeply shocked, slightly repulsed, even, by this revelation. I'm saying that so that you shan't think I'm one of those ladies myself. I wear ordinary female-looking clothes. I'm just a transvestite in disguise, and prefer to remain so. Or don't you agree?

Yes, I was slightly repulsed. But as you probably know, there is an attraction in every repulsion, so I couldn't take my eyes off her, either. Of course, these things changed later on, when young men started to grow their hair long and everyone started wearing unisex clothes, so that in the end no one knew which gender they fell in love with. But the relief that came from that confusion had to wait until years later. And later still, it has all gone back to normal. So again it's possible for real males to dress like real females and vice versa.

The ladies I am talking of were born at a time when they still had a chance of behaving like Real Males, and they had very deep voices accordingly. Whether this was due to beer and cigars or a suspect hormone that swam about in their bodies, I don't know. But one of them asked me to dance, and I said yes, grateful as I've always been when gentlemen rescue me from the disgrace of the wallflower. She held me tightly against her big, soft bosom and conducted me safely and authoritatively across the dance floor.

By and by a number of women came to our table and sat down. In the end there were two tables occupied by women and the remaining twenty by men. This was a men's place where women were curious deviants. The women all appeared to know each other. They embraced and said, 'How are you getting on?' and held each other round the waists – round the waists! – and seemed to be ever so glad to see each other.

Oh yes, it was a shocking place in every respect. But I was disappointed that so few of the famous whom I had always heard were queers weren't there. Where were all the actors with Adam's apples and famous artists with beards? At least I'd hoped to meet some interesting personalities. But what did I find? An assembly of secretaries, nurses, punch-card operators, shop assistants, librarians and teachers! A bunch of average people as average as average can be. What business did homosexuals have going around representing a normal sample of the population?

A couple of experienced ladies sat down and talked to Gunnhild and me, so that we shouldn't feel so isolated. We immediately started feeling a bit isolated. They at once assumed we were lovers. They didn't even ask. Everyone assumed that we were lovers, since we came together, and they referred to us the whole time as if we were a couple.

Now this was the first time that our relationship had been acknowledged by anyone but ourselves. Here we finally had the kind of acceptance we had longed and pined for all through our lonely months. And now we no longer wanted it. How were we to get out of this trap? Perhaps we would have to stay together for ever.

'How do you like it here?' asked a lady in a yellow silk blouse, a tight, black skirt and a necklace. (She was together with one of those ladies with cigars and hormones.)

'Well . . .' we said, self-consciously.

'Yes. But this is a place for surprises. Many of the members have met people here they'd never dreamed of meeting. Just you wait!'

This was promising. Fancy there being a chance of meeting people here whom one had met before. Prospects, prospects. We immediately thought suspiciously of everyone we knew.

'Do you know what happened today? Ingrid went to have her hair done this morning. And do you know who she met when she got here?'

'No.'

'The hairdresser!'

The ladies laughed heartily and cheered and kissed each other without embarrassment. Then they took on a more serious tone.

'How did you find out?' asked the lady in yellow silk.

This is simply one of the questions that follows you wherever you go. I have learned that now. You put it yourself some hours ago, before I launched into this monologue. It was one of the reasons I launched into it. Have you forgotten? Are you falling asleep? Oh, please don't fall asleep. A stupid question is better than none. But I assure you, next to the 'How do you do it' question, it is the most frequent question of all.

'How did you discover that you were a lesbian?'

But how did you discover your mother? How did you discover that you had big toes? How did you discover that you wanted food? How did you discover that you were there?

Did no one ask you those questions? But if someone asked them, what would you say? I am what I am? Yes. So am I.

I am what I am. But in my case it has to be discovered and explained. We are always put questions that we know as little about as you do. On our shoulders alone rests the burden of having to find answers to questions that are completely above us. Completely above everybody. How did we discover that we were lesbians? How do you discover a mountain when it rises up before you? How do you discover a tree full of blossoms when it stands there blooming in front of you? Do you have to explain what your eyes see and your ears hear and your heart feels?

You have the privilege of saying: I love her. No one asks why or how you know. That's the difference between us.

They simply ask: Does *she* love you? And you may answer yes or no. And you get applause or you get sympathy. That's the difference between us.

You love her and she loves you. You are together.

People ask: How are you getting on? You say: We are getting on beautifully. Or: We are getting on rather badly. And people say they're glad or they're sorry for you. But no one says, in the middle of your report on how your relationship is going: How did you discover the feelings that are the basis of this relationship? You don't have to talk about something else when what you need is sympathy and understanding for the situation you're actually in, or a piece of advice, perhaps. You are not put off the track. That's the difference between us. We always have to speak about *something else*.

We never get down to the roots of our troubles in this way. Even among ourselves we don't. Now the lesbian veterans were asking on our first evening at the club: How did you find out? What is your background? And they said: It's always the same story. And instead of refuting the question, we launched into explanations, relieved to be asked at all. It was the first time. At least here was a number of people taking it for granted that we were lesbians. But how come?

I was astonished that my background was so typical, and I wondered why I hadn't realised this before.

A domineering father and a submissive mother. Two sisters. At primary school I went to girls' classes and at secondary school I went to the language classes which were also crowded with girls. Since my father had never had a son, I became his hope of self-fulfilment.

It was crystal clear. There was only one way in which this could end up: I became a homosexual.

There are of course other reasons why one becomes a homosexual. The father-bond with its subsequent Electra complex is not at all the only explanation. If you have a domineering mother and a pale shadow of a father, female dominance at home will easily lead to an admiration for women and – even more unfortunate – female identification, with a corresponding contempt for the male, represented by one's father, the hen-pecked husband. Very many lesbians have had domineering mothers.

If one grows up alone with one's mother, the male will become a distant and peculiar figure, whom one will later have inhibitions approaching. The development of the personality will stagnate because of this strong mother-fixation and this will later possibly become a homophile component in the character structure. Several lesbians have had no father.

If one grows up in a family with only sisters, the intimacy

31

with them will easily lead to joint masturbation in the shared bedroom. This seemingly innocent deviation in behaviour may cause disturbances in natural mental growth, and one becomes a lesbian. It turns out that a lot of lesbians have had only sisters.

If one has only brothers, close contact with the male sex in the tender years will easily lead to the development of a nervous fear of all males, and one becomes a lesbian. A considerable number of lesbians have had only brothers.

If one grows up as an only child with one's father and mother, one will easily become spoilt, and therefore unsuited to the more mature role of women (which is that of self-sacrifice). The father will, moreover, tend to give his daughter the upbringing of a son, to compensate for the son he never had. Many fathers thus unknowingly exercise irreparable damage on their offspring. It turns out that the typical lesbian woman grew up as an only child.

If one grows up in an orphanage, the lack of safety and close contact with mother and father may lead to a failing ability to have natural, emotional relationships with other people – and one may seek refuge in immature and uncomplicated lesbian relationships. A great number of lesbians have spent their childhoods in orphanages.

It also turns out that parents may influence the development of lesbianism even before one is born. There are numerous stories of lesbians whose parents wanted a boy. When such parents have a girl, they do not face the truth and they pretend that they have a boy. And the poor innocent girl, of course, lives up to her parents' expectations, and becomes a lesbian – which in its turn causes the greatest of shocks to the parents.

Many personal tragedies could have been avoided if the parents had shown some sense of reality from the start, and immediately accepted their sonless state.

In normal families, however, daughters tend to become heterosexual.

Apart from a couple of cases in which a girl grows up with a father and a mother and two brothers and a sister. This is a dangerous and very complicated situation. In such cases there is a tendency towards sex polarisation in the home, such that the sisters have conspired against their two brothers and vice versa, and thereby developed an unfortunate solidarity with their own sex, which has later unwittingly been turned into lesbian love for other women. When one studies the matter more closely, one realises that there are actually an amazing number of lesbians who spent their childhoods with two brothers and a sister.

But these are all exceptions. In all other cases little girls grow up to become heterosexual women. That is, of course, also the normal state of affairs.

As I've already told you, I felt better as soon as I'd got all these things clarified.

FOUR

Kilroy was here

Suddenly I noticed that Gunnhild was getting deeper and deeper into conversation with the girl from the train. I became violently jealous. What business did the girl from the train have saying things that were worth listening to? But worse things were to come. About half an hour later they got up from their chairs simultaneously, as if there were some reticent understanding between them, and danced.

Now you may intervene and remind me that Gunnhild and I had decided to break up about a hundred times, but in the course of all that time there had not been the tiniest doubt in my soul that Gunnhild was my property. You may tell me that women are not supposed to feel like that, particularly not lesbian women, and I agree, of course, but I did. The moment I saw Gunnhild in the arms of another woman I had the most intense desire to have her back. I never ever got as close to being in love with her as I was then.

So what did I do? I couldn't very well go up to them, could I, and tap on their shoulders and say, 'Hey, you're dancing with my girl.' No. I looked around for someone suitable to take my revenge with. The lady with the cigars and hormones was now totally preoccupied with the girl in yellow silk and a necklace, and the two secretaries were laughing and kissing each other incessantly at another table. 'Helen', who was a real Helen, was dancing with a man several inches smaller than herself, and anyway, I didn't really see anyone around who could arouse my interest in *that* way. This was contrary to all experience. Mostly, as I said, I fall in love pretty easily, and there's always someone around in any crowd whom I find attractive. But here – at this clandestine meeting-place of the queers of Oslo – there was no one.

Apart from one of the secretaries, perhaps. But she was obviously violently married. In the following weeks I pondered much over this phenomenon. There were meetings at the club every fortnight, and we always went there, and Gunnhild and the girl from the train danced and talked and even started to have appointments elsewhere. This was not developing the way I wanted. Why didn't any of these girls attract me? It didn't seem as though I attracted any of them much either. So there we were, unattractedly looking at each other. Was perhaps the horrible truth that I could only fall in love with heterosexual women? Then what was I to do? Perhaps that was the well of loneliness.

Then came Agnes. Agnes was the *femme fatale* of the lesbian world, and I immediately decided that she was the girl for me. She immediately decided that I was the girl for her, too. Such things happen extremely quickly if they happen at all. It's the lesbian spark. Our fate was sealed to the tune of 'Climb Every Mountain', and by the time it reached its enchanting climax, ' . . . till you find your dream', we'd realised that we had to find another place. The sweetness of the music was mixed with the sweetness of Gunnhild's jealous glances, and Agnes and I disappeared triumphantly through the door.

We went home to her place, drank some Martini and went to bed. It wasn't very successful. That is, we were very much aroused and we made a big effort, but we never really got to the point of explosion. Nevertheless we pretended we'd exploded and assured each other with a series of voluptuous gasps. That's how we do it. Now you know.

35

We fell asleep, quite exhausted, and woke up late the next morning. It was wonderful to wake up beside her long, fair hair. I have always wanted to have long, beautiful hair myself, but then my hair is of the kind only suitable for relevant debate evenings.

Her bed was broad, the walls were red with posters saying 'Against Nuclear Weapons' and 'Norway out of NATO', 'Victory for FNL' and portraits of Fidel Castro. I was impressed that she'd taken her political consciousness into the bedroom. This was before it became fashionable to do so, and young people mostly had posters of bull-fighters and the Eiffel Tower on their walls. Everything about Agnes impressed me. If she'd said that she went in for the idea that Norway should re-conquer Greenland, I would have agreed on the spot.

There was also a series of photographs of girls on far-off beaches, and I recognised Agnes in most of them. This made me a bit uneasy, because it meant that others had been intimate with her before. I wanted Agnes to be my discovery.

In a corner was an enormous harp. And on the wall there was another stringed instrument I didn't recognise. We lay on our backs delighting in each other and having a cigarette, and I felt as wonderful as if I was in an advertisement for Marlboro. Yellow mountains, cacti and cowboys. This was freedom, peace and fulfilment – just as I was on the verge of disappearing down the well of loneliness.

'What instrument is that?' I asked, just to say something. By then we hadn't really said much.

'It's a lute.'

'Can you play it?'

'A little. Solveig can.'

'Solveig? Who is Solveig?'

'Ha! Solveig, who is Solveig? Kilroy, of course.

'I don't know anyone by the name of Kilroy.'

'Tell me, how long have you been going to the club?'

'Only since November . . .' I felt hopelessly naïve and left out.

'You've been there since November, and you mean to say that you don't know who Kilroy is? Didn't you see her yesterday?'

'I saw only you.'

I was deeply satisfied with my remark. Agnes smiled. Her smile was the kind that makes you pull a diamond out of your pocket, and say 'Do you want to come with me to Samarkand?' The soles of my feet tingled. I was just about to follow up my success, when Agnes said: 'Well, Solveig is the tall, fat woman with short, black hair and tight trousers. This is her flat.'

'Isn't it yours?'

'No, why should it be?'

No, why on earth should the flat that we went home to and slept in be hers?

'Just because I've been lying here thinking it was yours.'

She turned around and looked at me. I looked lovingly back.

'No, no, no. I'm just living here now. It's a temporary arrangement . . . I have to move out.'

'Why?'

'She is disappointed with me, she says. I went out with Marit, but it was just on the side. Solveig wasn't meant to know anything about it, but someone spied on us and told her, of course. I could wring her neck.'

'Whose neck?'

'Topsy's, of course. She came running at once and told Solveig everything, just because she loves to see Solveig furious. Besides, she wants Marit herself. Marit and Topsy had been together for a long time, and their relationship was quite miserable, and everyone at the club knew that, so they never called them anything but Topsy and Turvy. That serves them right. And Turvy, Marit that is, wanted to get away from Topsy, and fell in love with me. At first I said no, because I don't run away with other people's girls. But afterwards I realised that it was over, anyway, so I agreed. Topsy found us out. Turvy still lived with her, so we couldn't be together in her flat, and I lived with Solveig, so we couldn't be together in my flat, so we went to Helen's flat, but Helen's girlfriend immediately went and told Topsy, who went and told Solveig. She made a hell of a scene, Topsy that is, and called us whores and said there was no reason why the adultery commandment shouldn't be just as valid for homosexuals as for heterosexuals – she's in the Salvation Army, because then she can wear a uniform – and after this moral sermon she went straight to Solveig and told her everything. Solveig was furious. But she was also deeply wounded and disappointed. In spite of what had happened with Hedda.'

'Hedda?'

'Yes, Hedda. The bitch. Don't you even know who she is? Well, she once flirted with Solveig, and that wasn't the end of it. I forgave them, but it isn't the same the other way round.'

I was beginning to feel slightly uneasy. Here I was in the middle of a bed belonging to someone I didn't know, whose girl I had just been sleeping with, and whose nickname was Kilroy. Where was she? And wasn't it about time I got to my feet and disappeared into the blue?

'Where is Solveig now?' I said.

But it was too late. There was the sound of a key turning in a lock and a door being opened somewhere, and the foot steps of someone coming in and shutting the door. I stared wildly at Agnes. Where should I go? Hide under the carpet? Under the bed? In the cupboard? Jump out of the window?

'No, no, no,' said Agnes calmly. 'She won't kill you.' But I wasn't sure. I wasn't at all sure.

Sounds were now heard from the kitchen, the fridge was opened, calm and homely sounds, then foot steps approached our door. She flung the door open. She was big, almost fat, with her hair cut like a boy's at the neck. If I hadn't known by now that this must be Solveig, I would have thought it was a man. She appeared with a huge glass of milk in her hand. The milk in its calm innocence had a strangely provocative effect.

'What do you think you're doing?' she hissed.

'You see what I'm doing, don't you?'

'Don't I? Don't I? Do you know what I see?' She pointed with a furious finger towards the kitchen. 'I see that you haven't done the dishes for three days. That's what I see. And it was your turn this week. As long as you're living in my flat you have to stick to the rules we've agreed on, even if everything else has been smashed to pieces.'

She suddenly turned to me.

'Do you know something?'

I glanced at Agnes in confusion.

'No, I don't mean her, I mean you. You, the new little number there. Do you know something? She has lived here for six months, and all through that time she hasn't even touched the vacuum cleaner. She doesn't even know where it goes. Do you know where the vacuum cleaner goes, Agnes? I'm not only supposed to provide her with a place to live, but I have to earn money for her and be her housemaid and be betrayed by her, as well. Well. Please help yourself.'

Suddenly she changed her tone of voice. She came towards me with her hand outstretched. Whether it was sudden friendliness or irony was hard to decide. I took her hand hesitatingly.

'Good morning. My name is Solveig Bang. I see it as my duty to warn the town. You too. You have now become a part of town, too, you know. I can see that. Do you know how many girls have been seduced by this pretty little woman? Do you know how many women she has taken up lodgings with – in the name of love? And do you know how much money she has earned since she came to town? Not one single penny. But that's quite all right. Just lie there and drink my Martini. I don't mind. I don't mind at all.'

She marched out and slammed the door behind her. A moment later she opened it again and came running in, caught the Martini bottle that Agnes, who was standing beside the bed, had in her hand and hurled it to the floor roaring: 'Oh, yes, I do mind! I mind a hell of a lot. You steal everything. You steal everything I have. Everything!'

'Now you stop it, for heaven's sake!' I shouted. 'Are you mad?'

Agnes grasped my arm. 'Oh yes, she is. Don't do anything. You watch yourself.'

Solveig pointed to the bits of glass in the Martini pool on the floor.

'Now wipe it up! Wipe it up at once! Such a mess. How dare you make such a mess in my bedroom?'

'You made it yourself!' I shouted. But she was past reasoning, and Agnes said nothing. She just stared at her lamely.

'Now, won't you get a move on? Or perhaps you don't even know where the dustpan and brush go?'

'Honestly!' I said.

'Honestly, yes. I'll show you what's honest.'

She gave Agnes a violent push the moment she tried to rise from the bed, so she stumbled into the pool on her hands and knees. She started bleeding. I sprang to my feet and pushed Solveig aside. She stumbled into the harp, a discordant sound accompanying her shouts.

'Take it easy,' she shouted. 'I can manage both of you. That's no problem.' She took Agnes, wrung her arm and pushed her out the front door. Then she turned to me.

'You can't throw her out with no clothes on!' I said.

'Yes I can! And I can throw you out with no clothes, too.'

And so she did.

There we were at the top of the staircase, stark naked, with the temperature outside ten degrees centigrade. Agnes yelled and kicked the door. I asked her if she knew any of the neighbours; perhaps we could call them? She said the neighbours were fed up with her and Solveig because of all the girls' parties they'd had. I banged on Solveig's door.

'Give us our clothes, for god's sake.'

Not a sound from within. What were we to do? We couldn't go out into the street like this. Though perhaps it was the best solution, since then we would be arrested and taken to a warmer place. No, there must be some neighbour who could show some mercy, even if they were so unpopular. I suggested it again, but Agnes shook her head.

'Don't you understand that if they find out that we're having trouble again, Solveig will be thrown out of her flat?'

I couldn't really see that this was the time to consider Solveig, and advanced in the direction of the next door neighbour's flat. We couldn't stand there and half freeze to death.

Then Solveig's door opened just a fraction and we saw a hand throwing out some clothes. A moment later the door was opened once more and my bag flew through the opening. Then the door was slammed.

While we were dressing, we heard footsteps at the bottom of the staircase. An elderly gentleman was coming up the stairs. He stopped and stared. Then he pointed with his walking-stick at Agnes and said, 'Do you have to show yourself in public? My wife and I, we are elderly, respectable people. This is a disgrace for the whole building . . .'

Solveig's door was opened for the third time and two pairs of boots came flying through the air before she shut it. One of them landed just in front of the gentleman's newly polished shoe. 'Undressing-scenes on the stairs!' he gasped, retreating hastily back down the staircase.

FIVE

Digs strategy

This was the end of my first adventure at the club. You told me you wanted adventure stories, even though I said I didn't want to tell you. Soon you'll get the impression that this is how it is among lesbians. You'll run about town saying, lesbians are no better than other people. Meaning men. Men can beat their wives and raise hell and accuse them of being whores and flirtatious bitches. But no one ever raises his voice to say, that's typical hetero behaviour.

Now, the reason why I didn't really want to tell you my adventure stories is that I don't think you are mature enough for them. You draw the wrong conclusions the moment you hear them. Even lesbians themselves draw the wrong conclusions. They dislike such stories and hide them away in the cupboard. Every lesbian has a story in the cupboard. One that she doesn't know what to make of.

I don't know what to make of this myself. I just landed in it. I was witnessing the end of a tragedy. I came into it in its last scene. And my own little role in it was not one to be particularly proud of.

But there I was – with a heroine who had just come off-stage. I felt as though I had rescued her, even though the rescue wasn't very heroic, and the audience not exactly ideal for my performance. But still, I don't want you to think that lesbian relationships are normally like this. In Paris they are, of course. And in London there are clubs specially for women all over the place, packed with lesbians who get into intrigues the moment they step inside. And in Copenhagen they share in the broad currents of European culture as always, so every time they have a so-called girls-only evening, all the girls throw themselves into fist fights, smash the furniture in western saloon style, steal each other's girlfriends and take LSD. But in Oslo we're a bit backward.

Agnes and I went home to my place in a taxi. At the time I still rented a room from an elderly married couple, the room with a view of the wall and the pigeons, and I was forbidden to have male visitors after ten o'clock in the evening. The moment I moved in I had been informed that they were very old-fashioned in this respect, and my landlady said, 'Such affairs simply make Mr Christoffersen see red.'

I had asked her if I could perhaps have female visitors.

'Oh, that's different, of course. Quite different. But male visitors,' my landlady repeated, 'that's where Christoffersen draws the line.'

When we got home, I boiled some eggs and made tomato soup. Eggs tend to calm your nerves, don't you think? Do you want some eggs? Shall I boil an egg for you while I continue my story? Or aren't your nerves on edge? Yes, I thought so. Agnes and I glanced self-consciously at each other while I boiled the eggs and made the tomato soup. Doing practical things is awkward when one has hitherto only done romantic things. Like dancing, smiling, embracing and looking beautiful. I imagine my beauty fades a bit when I make soup. And I desperately wanted Agnes to find me beautiful.

Now apart from these trivial matters that had to be attended to, the episode we had just been through had of course also destroyed some of our new-born bliss. But I decided to forget about it. I decided that Solveig was a brutal monster, who indeed deserved her nickname, and that all the

43

things she had said about Agnes were lies. But deep down in my heart a voice said to me, *What she can do to Solveig, she can do to you.*

I immediately silenced this voice, and went on with my tomato soup. Agnes was standing right beside me, and just the nearness of her made me quiver with happiness. Foolishly happy, I divided out the soup. I was proud I'd found such a rose in the depths of the underworld.

Agnes had moved in. There was no doubt about it. After we'd lived at my place for about a week, I could bear the sneaking up and down stairs and in and out of rooms no longer, so I went straight to Mrs Christoffersen and told her how things were. That is, I didn't tell her how things were at all. I said I had a friend, who was looking for a room to rent and had no place to stay in the meantime. Could she live with me for a while? Mrs Christoffersen asked a lot of questions which were all answered evasively or mendaciously and she promised to lay the matter before Christoffersen himself.

Christoffersen had the following view of this matter when it had been presented to him: on condition that it was a strictly temporary arrangement and that the rent was raised by 50 kroner per month (I already paid kr. 200) because of an increase in wear on the carpets, use of the bathroom, increased disturbances as a result of more voices being heard, as well as his general conviction that no person should live cost free (they themselves paid kr. 173 to the proprietor for the whole flat), my friend was allowed to stay. Mrs Christoffersen repeated 'strictly temporary' four or five times as if the expression was a kind of charm, and said that Christoffersen had indicated that it meant till the end of April.

Then there was the bed. Mrs Christoffersen really thought of everything. They had a portable steel-spring thing with folding legs in the attic, she told me. We should by all means use it. It was really no trouble at all, because they never used

44

it, anyway. As a matter of fact, she could show us where it was and help us bring it down.

Agnes and I, who had been sleeping wonderfully in my broad bed the whole week, smiled and said that it was really not necessary. Oh yes, dear, come along, I'll just get the key.

So we trotted off to the attic and got the bed out and said it was indeed very thoughtful of her and thank you very much and she shouldn't have taken the trouble.

This was not the worst. We naturally clapped the bed together and squeezed it under the other one and slept as we'd done before. At that time Agnes and I had not yet found each other, I mean sexually, if you see what I mean. But that evening we had got into bed really quickly and found each other wonderfully. If you see what I mean. Just at the point where I was about to arrive at the summit of pleasure, where one just doesn't give a damn, there was a knock at the door.

Good gracious! The door wasn't locked. We saw the handle being moved downwards.

'Just a moment!' I screamed. 'We've already gone to bed!' I added hysterically in a voice that was better suited to a fire warning.

Mrs Christoffersen's voice was heard from outside. 'Don't worry, dear, I'm not at all fussy.'

'Just a minute,' I implored.

If only I hadn't been so foolish as to announce that we'd already gone to bed. In total confusion we dragged out the steel-spring thing and tried to get it on its legs in a hurry, but it wasn't of a kind that I'd been exposed to before, so at first we couldn't find out how to unfold it and we pulled the same bed legs in opposite directions at the same time, and I called to Mrs Christoffersen in a distressed voice that we were almost ready. But what on earth we were supposed to be almost ready with, from her point of view, was rather unclear. At long last the bed stood on its legs in the corner with blankets and sheets and everything, but without a mattress. We had forgotten about the mattress, it was still lying under my bed. We lay down in our beds.

'You can come in now,' I called encouragingly.

Mrs Christoffersen marched in and clapped her hands.

'Oh dear, how practically you've arranged everything,' she said. 'Just fancy that. Actually I didn't think there was enough room for a bed in the corner. I thought the two beds would have to be standing side by side. But it's much more convenient this way, of course. Then you don't have to breathe right into each other's faces and so on. . . if you see what I mean.'

We nodded and stared at her. As for her, she stared more and more intensely at Agnes's bed. Then she ventured to lift the sheet a bit.

'But, dear, didn't you get the mattress? Where on earth did I put it? I'm quite sure there was a mattress to go with that bed. . . if you see what I mean.'

'But we did get a mattress, didn't we, Agnes?' I said, as if this remark served to make the situation any better.

'Oh dear,' exclaimed Mrs Christoffersen with the joy of recognition, pointing under my bed. 'There it is!'

'Yes,' said Agnes. 'But I prefer a hard bed.'

'Well, but on those springs?. . . if you see what I mean.'

At this point Agnes demonstrated a resourcefulness of which I must admit I hadn't thought her capable. So I was almost taken in when she suddenly said, 'You see, I practise deep meditation. One should be able to withstand certain physical trials.'

'Oh dear, are you an ascetic?'

'Not exactly. . .'

'Just fancy that,' Mrs Christoffersen said and made herself comfortable on the side of the bed. 'Because Mr Christoffersen himself is so interested in astrology and the stars.'

Before we knew how to stop her, she had plunged into a

long monologue with us.

You may be wondering why she came at all. I must admit I've been wondering about that myself. Who knows? Perhaps she forgot why she really came. Because she certainly didn't tell us. Or was the thing that she certainly didn't tell us only a subterfuge? Or was Mrs Christoffersen really a lesbian?

This is one of the many questions that will never be fully answered.

SIX

Strangers in the night

Now there is undoubtedly something called lesbian humour. It doesn't arise from our hormones or from some other malformation of body and soul, but from the absurdity of situations we find ourselves in. You see, the reason why you managed not to laugh all through the preceding story is that you don't see this absurdity. You expect something else. You expect me to be deadly serious. Perhaps titillating. But serious. Did you ever read a funny story about people in wheelchairs? Would you be prepared to read a funny story about people in wheelchairs, if you came across one? No. People in wheelchairs are not supposed to have a sense of humour. They are not supposed to have a sense of absurdity. Nor are lesbians.

Deviants of any kind are supposed to sit tight lamenting their situation and never noticing the absurdity of things.

Now it may be that you didn't laugh simply because my story wasn't funny. But it was. Perhaps you're a boring listener. Did you like your egg? I'm glad. After all, nothing can move a woman's heart more than having cooked a perfect egg. You want to hear more about Agnes?

The relationship between Agnes and me was a really good one. We never quarrelled. Actually, I get on better sexually with people I also quarrel with. But that's because I'm a pervert.

During this period I tried desperately to make up for my lost young love life. I plunged into a kind of belated adolescence and went hand in hand with Agnes wherever we went. It couldn't really be a great triumphal march through town, of course, since no one we passed seemed to share our bliss. So it became a kind of march of defiance instead. A stubborn romance. When we were taking long walks in the fields and forests we were much freer. The pines and the sun had nothing against our happiness. But once a human being turned up our hands slid automatically from each other; we were so fed up with strange glances. Once a man with a fresh and sporty face stopped on his jogging round and glared, and turned round as we passed. Then he shook his head and said, 'Well, the war is responsible for many strange things.'

We lived a very hectic life. We went around to all the cafés and restaurants and meeting-places where there was the slightest chance of seeing other gays, and of course we went to the club every fortnight.

Agnes and I had nothing in common. Our only commonly-shared interest was beer-drinking. But the thing was, I was astonished that I could get hold of someone so pretty. You see, I have always accepted the beauty scale. According to this scale you always have to find someone who is on the same level of beauty as yourself. If you have a rather broad behind and dandruff you jolly well have to find a pear-shaped person with a podgy face and a potato nose. If you have wispy hair, you jolly well have to find someone else with wispy hair. And if you don't find anyone, it serves you right; it's no wonder you can't find someone when you have such wispy hair. And if you run away with that beautiful woman who has Sunsssiiilk in her hair and who is walking along the beach in the summer breeze, I'll be wondering why on earth she chooses you. You look as if you don't even know what Sunsilk is. I mean, one has to have a sense of reality. And this is the state of affairs among lesbians too. No difference. Absolutely no difference.

Therefore I shouldn't really have been going around with Agnes, because she belonged to a level on the beauty scale far higher up than my own. With the result that I imagined for a long time that I was really two levels prettier than I am.

We had a great time at the club. I couldn't stand it when Agnes was talking to Turvy, and Topsy couldn't stand it when Turvy talked to Agnes, and Agnes and Turvy were offended when Topsy and I danced with each other, and all four of us looked through Solveig as if she were thin air, and everybody had somebody who they looked through and danced merrily past as if they were thin air, and laughed and cheered and shouted, 'What a jolly good time we had last Sunday!' melting together with their hearts' delights to the tune of 'Strangers in the Night'.

I went into fits of jealousy one day when Agnes finally spoke to Solveig, and avenged myself by dancing cheek to cheek with Gunnhild. But when Solveig and Agnes started dancing, too, Hedda rushed at Agnes and smacked her face, and Solveig went off like a rocket and squeezed Hedda's arm until she started screaming, and the menfolk rushed up and down the stairs shouting, 'Hey, there's a fight upstairs!' and came running in to watch and nudged each other and said, 'Isn't it horrid?' while Topsy and Turvy tried to split the three of them up. Afterwards they got blamed for the whole hullaballoo.

That night Agnes disappeared with Solveig. She didn't even say goodbye. Suddenly she just wasn't there. I lay waiting for her all night, but in the end I was forced to realise I was defeated. The woman obviously had a sexual radiation that I couldn't compete with.

But in spite of this realisation I went over to Solveig's place the next day. I sat for hours outside her door. No, I sat on the corner, so that I couldn't be seen. I saw Agnes as a kind of prisoner whom I had to set free. I could think of nothing else

50

to do. When hours had passed, someone came out of the front door. It was Solveig. She went in the opposite direction, so I ran up to Solveig's door and rang the bell. Nobody answered. 'Agnes! I know you're there. Please let me in. We have to talk,' I said. No answer. In the end I had to go. I went into town, down-hearted. Why did I humiliate myself so? Wasn't it a clear message? Why was I so desperate to get Agnes back? I knew I couldn't have a lasting relationship with someone like her. We were miles apart in every respect. Except for the beer, as I mentioned. Still, I was in love with her, and I couldn't get her out of my system.

I went home. There was a message for me under my door. 'Hello, dear. I love you. Don't be angry with me. Please. I'll come tonight. Agnes.'

Joy flooded through my empty brain. She kept her word. She came, she loved me, and she went away. In this way she kept me paralysed for several weeks. I never thought of anything but whether she would come or not. I hardly ventured out of my dreadful digs, just because I was afraid she would come when I wasn't there. I sat staring desperately at the telephone for hours on end. I still went to the club every fortnight in the hope of seeing her. Sometimes she came, sometimes she didn't. Sometimes she danced with me and seemed to be just as much in love with me as before. But when Solveig was there, she looked right through me. Agnes was the most exciting woman I had ever met in my life.

Suddenly one day Mrs Christoffersen asked, 'What about Miss Svane? Doesn't she live here any more?'

No, Mrs Christoffersen. Miss Svane has broken it off with me, Mrs Christoffersen. Broken it off. Do you understand? She is with another woman now, Mrs Christoffersen. She is keeping me on a string, you see? Sad? Yes, one could call it that. But that's how it is in our world too. No difference. Absolutely no difference.

'No. She's found another place to stay, now.'

'Well. I hope she's found a good place.'

'Yes, it's fine . . .'

'Has she got her own flat, perhaps?'

'Yes, she's moved into a flat.'

'That's amazing, considering the housing shortage.'

'Yes, it's quite amazing . . .'

When I had thus finally told Mrs Christoffersen the truth and the rent was accordingly reduced by kr 50, Agnes came back. She seemed exhausted and worn out, but I was happy. I'd been convinced the whole time that it was really me she preferred, and she stuck to Solveig only because Solveig was a bully.

She told me that Solveig had walked out on her.

All these calamities didn't scare us away from the club, however. On the contrary, they were like a magnet drawing us to the field of battle. What would happen next? In any case, Agnes and I were both at a point in our lives when we found such troubles inspiring despite the knowledge that such times are usually periods of depression.

Solveig, Topsy and Turvy, Gunnhild, Hedda, Sofie (the girl on the train) and all the others who played some part in our drama were at the same stage during that time. So we kept on meeting the same clique.

One Saturday evening in early spring the inevitable happened. Gunnhild and Solveig made their grand entrance – one hour later than usual – hand in hand, obviously in an atmosphere of love requited. For a second time I experienced acute pangs of jealousy, but this time I must admit I was also scared. Should I warn her? On the other hand, the eighth commandment is one of the two commandments that I always keep. I don't believe in bearing false witness against my neighbour, and what did I know about the background of what Solveig had done that day? I decided to say nothing. Gunnhild would find out Solveig's true nature in due course, and if it was as wicked as I had seen, I would help Gunnhild out then.

Agnes and I consequently made a great pretence of treating them as if they were thin air. 'Strangers in the Night' thundered out of the loudspeakers. It's a tune especially well suited to ignoring past lovers and melting into the arms of your present one. 'Love was just a glance away, a warm embracing dance away – jubi-dubi-doo, oh, jubi-doobee . . .' – but then, lo and behold, Gunnhild and Solveig came straight up to us and said they thought it was foolish to go on ignoring each other, when we did, after all, know one another.

So we were trapped. They planned a party. It should be given at Topsy and Turvy's place, because the time was perhaps – ha, ha – not yet ripe to have it in the flat belonging to Kilroy herself. A big party. A bunch of Danish lesbians would come up on the boat from Copenhagen, too. Lone and Jette and the others. It would be grand.

'Well, yes, thank you very much,' we said, and smiled. 'So nice of you to invite us,' we said. And then we stared enviously after them as they glided into the last notes – and kissed each other long and intensely just at the point where it changes key: 'Ever since that night, we've been together, *lovers* at first sight, in love for ever. *It turned out so right for strangers in the night.*'

SEVEN

Oh, let's live together as sisters*

Did you ever attend a lesbian orgy? Didn't you? No? The first precondition for attending a lesbian orgy is that you are a lesbian. Which of course you aren't. So few people are lesbian. Mention five! No? You can't mention five? But statistically five percent of the population are homosexual. Don't you know even a hundred people?

Shakespeare wasn't a lesbian either. Apart from that, there are many remarkable stories about him. But a lesbian? No. Elizabeth I, on the contrary, had strong lesbian propensities. Anyway, that's what historians keep speculating about. She was, for example, unmarried. And that is a circumstance that one has often, after closer studies in the field, found utterly suspect. Particularly in women. Not to mention queens – who ought to bear male children for the sake of the throne.

But on the whole one hasn't bothered much to study the field in this respect. And why should one? One would risk crushing the myth of the indispensability of the male – the ruler and lord. That would be extremely dangerous. He would risk becoming merely an equal.

*The Norwegian national psalm says, 'Oh, let us live together as brethren, as Christians it's good and right.'

Back to the orgy that you're waiting so eagerly to hear about. Now you're waiting not only to hear how two women do it when they do it, but how dozens and dozens of women do it when they do it. We are approaching the core of the forbidden fruit. Because, of course, lesbians aren't satisfied with just one bite of the apple. They eat it to the core. And they're not expelled from paradise.

But since the rest of mankind has been expelled, there's no one left to watch us. So, I'm sorry to say, our orgies must remain a secret. Their very core is secrecy. Therefore studies in the field hardly ever lead to anything. It isn't the right field that one is studying. And still there was no voice being heard in the garden calling, 'Eve, where art thou?'

But who cares? She is, of course, with *him*. Everyone knows that. Therefore she is never asked. But *if* . . . it's just an hypothesis, *if* she isn't with him, where is she? Well then, she is simply not there.

I am tired of being not there.

But now for the orgy. Can you hear sounds in the distance? Your entry ticket: an artificial penis in your luggage. Yes, here it reappears, this archetypal image which has dominated our civilisation since the spirit of Freud moved upon the face of the waters. We grasp it tenderly in our voluptuous and greedy hands.

Once we're inside the dive, we climb on top of each other. Everyone. In a heap. And then we start doing it. We do it and we do it. I'm sorry to use a circumlocution here. But you know what I mean. *It*.

Disgusting? Are you saying it's disgusting? I agree. I couldn't agree more. But what did you expect a lesbian orgy to consist of? A milk and honeycake party at Donald Duck's grandmother's?

Truly I say unto you, you can't ever know what a lesbian orgy is like.

Nor will the journalist ever know, the one who wrote an

article in *Dagbladet* about a big homosexual orgy in Johannesburg that had been raided by the police. 'There were also two ladies present at the party. The police have not succeeded in finding out what the two ladies were doing there . . .'

As I said, the great union of brethren was going to take place. Or which word should I use? The great union of sisters? As if women can be sisters. It sounds preposterous. 'Oh, let us live together as sisters, as Christians it's good and right.' Our national hymn is so beautiful. I mean it. I've always sung it with a lump in my throat. You mustn't think I'm anything but a sweet, little Norwegian girl with ribbons in my hair and a flag. After all lesbians celebrate 17 May too.*

Well, it may not be good and right, but they do. But it's only good and right as long as one doesn't know anything about it. As long as one stands there, waving flags at the children, not knowing that there's a lesbian going past celebrating the independence of the nation, it's all very good and right.

But now we're getting off the point. Where is our lesbian orgy? It disappeared. You must admit that nowadays progress progresses so fast that everyone accepts homosexuality; in fact, it's becoming slightly unfashionable not to accept homosexuality, and to be unfashionable – that's the deadliest thing one can be. No, homosexuality is accepted, in my opinion. There is no doubt about it. So why all this fuss? Homosexuality – but that's really a private matter. What people do in their beds – or out of them, if that's what they prefer – it's no business of mine.

*17 May is Constitution Day in Norway when everyone celebrates the nation as a free and independent state. It is a great national feast, with songs in the streets, ice-cream for the children and speeches about freedom. Everyone dresses up in her best clothes and goes into the streets with flags. [Translator's note]

So back to our little private matter: the big lesbian feast of sisterhood that was to happen at Topsy and Turvy's place on the following Saturday. We'll let it remain a private matter. I refuse to give you any account of our party.

Today, dear friends, I'd rather talk about the importance of the account that wasn't there. That's what I've been wanting to talk about the whole time.

Here it is:

EIGHT

Eve, where art thou?

NINE

The lie of loneliness

At this point in my odyssey as a new-born lesbian I got a message from my aunt asking me to come and stay with her for a week in her house on the outskirts of Oslo. The family who was occupying the first floor was going away on holiday, and she didn't like being in the house alone. I had done this a couple of times before, and I went off this time, too, even though it was painful to think it meant a week's separation from Agnes. A week was a very long time in those days.

But I had my books, of course. I was a student, remember, and, although you may not have got this impression, I was studying all through the heroic events of this story.

So I took my books and went off to my aunt, who is a great talker and a marvellous storyteller, and it was really a relaxing time away from everything. Fortunately the family upstairs came back two days early because of bad weather in the mountains – gale and hail the whole time. Ending your life in such gales is a common pastime for holiday makers in Norway, but this family didn't intend to die just yet. So they came back and I took the tram back to my digs in town, delighted at the thought of seeing Agnes again. When I got home, I was pretty thirsty, so I went into the kitchen and helped myself to a big glass of milk. Then I went to my room. There was Agnes lying in my bed, as I had expected. But she wasn't alone. On the pillow beside her I recognised the short, fair hair of the girl from the train.

Never in my life did my IQ fall so rapidly down to zero. The room was a mess. There were bottles and dirty glasses and plates with congealed gravy and potatoes all over the place, clothes in every corner, overflowing ashtrays and stuffy air.

'What the hell do you think you're doing?' I said, slowly drinking my milk.

'I didn't expect you home till Sunday,' she said.

'And that means you can mess up the place to your heart's delight, and take other women into my bed?'

'I was going to clean up,' said Agnes faintly.

'Clean up!' I muttered. 'You don't even know where the vacuum goes.'

She looked at me with her beautiful eyes. 'Out!' I screamed. 'Get out! I don't want you. I never wanted you! It's just a game. It doesn't mean a thing to you.'

They both got up and started dressing. I sat down and watched. My IQ was rising slowly. What was I up to? Agnes was now fully dressed and she stood in front of me. The girl from the train had just slipped out the door without a word. There was a crucial moment of silence.

'Agnes,' I said, 'don't go. Please don't go.'

'I must,' she said. 'Sofie is waiting for me.'

Sofie? Oh yes. I always forgot that the girl from the train had a name. But what did she have to do with Agnes and me?

'We have to talk,' I said. 'We can't go on like this. Tell her to go away. Make some other date with her. We must talk.'

'But we'd planned. . .'

'To hell with what you'd planned!' I interrupted at the top of my voice.

Agnes went away and came back. We sat opposite each other saying nothing for a long time. Then I said, 'You don't love me, Agnes, do you?'

'I love your thoughts.'

I was puzzled by her answer. My thoughts! What did she know about my thoughts? I wanted her to love my face, to love my body. I wanted her to think I was beautiful. I didn't want her to love my thoughts.

'What about yourself?' she said. 'Do you love me?'

No, I thought. No – I didn't really think so. It was just a sound that came into my head. No.

'I love your face,' I said. 'I think you're beautiful.'

'I don't want that,' she said. 'I want you to love what's inside.'

But what was inside her? I stopped to think; I hardly knew anything of what was inside Agnes.

Again we were quiet. Here we were. I wanted to be loved for my looks and was loved for my brains; she wanted to be loved for her brains and was loved for her looks. We loved each other for all the wrong reasons. Was it love? What is love?

'I don't really think you love me at all,' she said.

'We use the word too much,' I said. I didn't want to admit it. What was the point of anything, if I didn't love her? I wanted to love her. But I knew what love was. I had loved Tove. This wasn't it. But I would rather die than admit it.

'I don't love you either,' she said. 'I've never loved you.'

I looked up at her. It was a strange relief, even though I was hurt. She had had the courage to touch the taboo, the real taboo between us: that we didn't love each other. Even though we were lesbians. And what's the point of being a lesbian if one doesn't love?

'No,' I said. 'You love Solveig, don't you?'

'Yes.'

'But how can you love someone who abuses you?'

'It's a long story,' said Agnes.

But she told it.

This is Agnes's story. Do you want to hear it? It's a sad story. And it's not at all the kind of story you wanted to hear when you asked how two women do it. The only thing you thought about was: after all, it's against nature. No children come out of it. So what's the point? Is sexual intercourse with a condom against nature? Or a diaphragm? Or the pill? Would you say so? May I tell you the story of Agnes even though it's not about copulation at all?

OK. I'll make it brief. Agnes was poor. She had no mother and no father. She grew up in a tiny place in the valleys called Ringebu. It's a beautiful place, with high mountains rising everywhere and a strong river running through it. But it's impossible to be a lesbian there. You know, the more beautiful the landscape is, the more hopeless it is to be a lesbian in it. One has to be a lesbian in ugly cities like Oslo. You don't think Oslo is ugly? That's just because it's so beautiful once you get out of it. But anyway, Agnes came to Oslo – with no money, no job and no education. She got odd jobs that she didn't like. Her real dream was to become an actress. That was impossible. Then she met Solveig. Solveig had a good job in a business firm, she had a flat, and she was good to her. Solveig was the first person in the world who really wanted her. But they didn't agree about domestic things. Solveig wanted a tidy place and Agnes wanted a messy one. They quarrelled. Solveig got into the habit of beating her. Once she had started, she couldn't get out of it.

You don't want me to go on? Why not? I don't really want to go on either. But what is it that makes us shrink from the thought of women being brutal? Men are brutal all over the world. They fight and they drink and scream. It's horrible. But it's not considered inappropriate.

Now I didn't invite you here to tell you a pack of lies, but the truth is inappropriate. Agnes's story is the most inappropriate story I know. But it's there. Why is there no place for it?

They went to a psychiatrist. Solveig also wanted to get out of her bad habits. She was unhappy. Her father had taught her to defend herself against the boys when she was a small girl. She knew how to box. She grew up in one of the poorest districts of Oslo.

The psychiatrist was an unprejudiced man. He treated them as if they were a perfectly normal married couple. Agnes sat there at his table with a bruised eye and a swollen nose. The psychiatrist said, 'But you love each other, don't you?' They nodded. 'Love is the most important thing,' said the psychiatrist. 'Once you have decided to stick together, you should try and carry it through. What are your dreams?'

He asked each of them for their dreams. They told him their dreams. They were mostly absurd pictures that didn't make sense, but the psychiatrist nodded thoughtfully without letting them know what he made of them. Then he said to Agnes, 'Do you have a fear of men?' 'No,' she answered, without knowing what that had to do with anything. 'Do you have a fear of male genitals?' the psychiatrist asked. 'No,' said Agnes again. 'I don't think of them very often.'

Then the psychiatrist turned to Solveig and asked her the same questions. And then it seemed that the consultation was over.

'But. . .but. . .' said Agnes.

The psychiatrist raised his eyebrows. 'But?'

Agnes raised her hands. 'I'm afraid she'll kill me!'

The psychiatrist was a very handsome man with black hair and intense, warm brown eyes. Now he turned his handsome face to Solveig. 'Is that so?'

'Yes,' said Solveig. 'That's so. I get so mad that I could kill her. I lose my wits completely. I don't know what I'm doing. I just see a mass of red. Her face becomes blurred, I don't see anything clearly. I just hit and hit, and I might easily beat her to death one day, because I don't know what I'm doing.'

'She needs help,' said Agnes hopefully, since he'd let her

63

make this whole speech of confession without interruption. 'Couldn't she get a place at a mental hospital or something?'

The psychiatrist looked at Solveig.

'You're young and strong and healthy. You surely don't want to go to a mental hospital, do you?'

'Yes,' said Solveig. 'Or, at least, I want someone to help me. Can no one help me?'

The psychiatrist frowned. Then he leaned back and looked out of the window. 'You know, a little quarrelling happens in the best of families. If people went to hospital for treatment on these grounds, half the Norwegian population would be in hospital.'

And that was that. That was the story.

I was sitting there, listening to Agnes's story. I didn't want to believe it. I didn't want to think about it at all. I said, 'You must get away from her.'

She said, 'Yes. That's what I'm trying to do.'

'So you were only with me to get away from her?'

'In a way, yes. And when you went away to your aunt, Solveig came to take me home. She seeks me out everywhere. She says she'll kill me if I don't stay with her. So I ran away from her and fetched Sofie, and that's why we were here. I can't be alone. Then she comes to get me.'

'But that's madness.'

'Yes. But it's a madness that's obviously accepted in this bloody world.'

'Can't you stay with me?'

'You said you didn't want me.'

'I never said. . .'

Oh yes. I had said that. That's what I had been shouting at her just about an hour ago. There was some truth in it, I knew. There is always some truth in such shouting.

'I'll go to Ringebu,' said Agnes.

'But do you have anyone there?'

'Yes. There's a married couple I can stay with.'

So Agnes went to Ringebu. She left a few days later. I took her to the railway station. Spring was coming. We said goodbye and we kissed, disregarding the glances of those who were kissing normally around us. I went along the quay by the fjord towards the Castle of Akershus, rising, flood-lit, above the water. The most beautiful part of Oslo. Women don't walk there alone and at a slow speed at such an hour. I realised what had happened. I was more alone than ever. I had thought that by contacting the Society of 1948 I would break out of my isolation. Instead I had broken into it. There was a wall around us. We couldn't break through it. Even when we were together we couldn't break through it. Nobody dared to gather outside the walls.

How could anyone love anyone in such a stuffy atmosphere? No wonder we didn't love each other when we never got enough air to breathe. You're fussing about the lesbian movement. What the hell is that? you're saying. What's the point of a lesbian movement? Do you want all the world to become lesbians?

Oh, little do you know of the lesbian movement. This was years before anyone even thought of a lesbian movement. But its core lies here. In the lies that we told each other because we wanted so desperately to be happy. We were crammed together because there was no room for us elsewhere, just like people in a ghetto. If you want to get out of the ghetto, you have to fight.

But everywhere we were told that we were perverts and freaks of nature. You're even saying it now, after all these years. At that time a psychologist appeared in Oslo, and wrote interesting articles in the paper about how to cure homosexuality. He had been in the United States for eight years and in the course of those years he had cured a number of homosexual males of their illness.

Just fancy! He'd succeeded in curing some people of their love for other people! But then it had taken him quite a long time. Eight years of his life had been devoted to this cause. But not in vain. He had at least succeeded in curing some homosexuals of their love for psychologists.

He had succeeded in keeping us in our place. Within the walls, where we can try and swallow his lies about us. The lie of loneliness: that we are sick people, and that the society where people are free to practise such perverted theories as his is sane.

This man is a pervert. He wants to change nature. He wants to change the natural growth of love between a woman and a woman, or between a man and a man. If society itself wasn't hostile to love, he would never have been allowed to do that. Can't you see? Why can't you ever get it out of your head that love is against nature? Because that's what you're saying when you say homosexuality is against nature. Didn't nature make me? Or was I a result of some mysterious embryonic experiment, conceived on another planet, and planted in my mother's womb? Because I can assure you: I was *born* a lesbian. I was lesbian the moment I came out and said, Boooooo.

And I grew up, and I became strong and healthy and full of life. I saw the flowers grow and I saw the beautiful sky and I fell in love. I held her hand and I was fourteen years old. Everything I was lived in that grasp. Life was wonderful and I was never going to die.

This is what they want to cure me of. And because they want to cure me and because I don't want to be cured, I seek refuge in a place where no flowers grow and where you can't see the sky, and I don't fall in love. I seek desperately for someone to hold hands with, and I hold one hand after the other, pretending that all that I am lives in that grasp, and that life is wonderful and that I never want to die. But I do. I do want to die. I want to get out of this hell of a place. But who can help me? Can no one help me?

No. I have to help myself. I have to find others who think

the same thoughts as me. Together we'll have to break out, whether we love each other or not. And in doing so, perhaps we'll start loving, too.

That's how it is.

TEN

Try my prick, won't you?
(a normal intermezzo)

Where was I? Yes, I was standing by the Castle of Akershus watching its beautiful flood-lit image reflected in the fjord. A little foolish figure at the City Hall Square who accepted that she was lied to.

I don't want to conceal the fact that I am an intelligent person; it's only the things I do that are foolish. But my thoughts are wise.

Now, for example, I had the wise thought that I couldn't stand it any longer. I wouldn't accept that people 'didn't know about me', as the saying goes. 'Hello! Ho-mo!' I would break out, even if I had to be alone doing it. I'd come out, as it's called. Since I'd become aware of myself – as we who have become aware of ourselves usually put it – other people jolly well had to realise that I was *like that*. Hey, hey – I'm one of the 'friends'. Are you? Or to put it frankly, I have certain propensities. Or even more precisely, I'm one of the family.

This was the end. With great determination I went up the street towards the National Theatre. I noticed that a man had started walking right behind me. I reacted at once. I didn't react by walking more quickly, as ladies ought to do in such situations. Oh, no. I turned quickly towards him.

He was a young man with a coat and tie – a couple of years

older than me, perhaps. He looked a bit abashed, but smiled encouragingly. 'Come for a drink?' he asked.

'I'm sorry. I'm not at all interested in men. You see, I'm a lesbian,' I said.

I lost courage the moment the words were said. After all, this was the first time I'd said them, and I was on the brink of playing the role of the clown.

'What-did-you-say-you-were?' he asked.

There was still a chance to get out of it.

'A lesbian. That means that I'm interested in women, not in men.'

'Oh . . .'

I started walking again. He came quickly after me and touched my arm. I turned around again quickly.

'Didn't you hear what I said?'

'Yes, but don't you like beer?'

'Yes, I love beer, and I drink beer every day.'

'Well, then, you can drink one with me, can't you?'

'I can, if you realise that it doesn't mean I'm going to bed with you.'

'Don't talk nonsense!'

'Why shouldn't I talk nonsense, when it's not?'

'Come on, let's talk. Just talk . . .'

We went to the Kaba Restaurant. I ordered a pint, and another one and another one. He insisted on paying for them, and in this he was in secret collusion with the waiter. But I insisted on paying myself.

I got tipsy. I told him I'd just said goodbye to my girlfriend at the railway station, and that I was sad. He said he was studying law and planned to take his final exam in the autumn, and that his girlfriend had let him down that day. She was supposed to meet him outside the Rainbow Night Club, but she hadn't turned up. He asked what kind of males I'd been exposed to, since I preferred girls. I asked him the same question.

'But that's not the same thing,' he said.

'Why not?'

'Because . . . because . . .' he said. That was his way of saying 'But I am a man'. 'But I am a man' is always a good argument.

'You ought to be the first person to understand why I like girls when you're sitting here flirting with me. I'm jealous of you.'

'Jealous?'

'Yes, because you're lucky enough to be together with a girl just now. That's actually the real reason why going to bed with men makes me so sad. Not that I'm indifferent to them. But that I envy them, because they're holding a woman in their arms.'

He smiled a bit askew. He was rather sweet. That was really the worst thing about it, because then I couldn't help being a little bit nice to him. And this niceness is always misunderstood, no matter what I actually say. I don't know what's the matter with me.

'Do you know something?' he said, stretching his hand across the white tablecloth. 'You're sweet. You're the kind of girl who becomes sweeter the more one looks at you.'

There it was. The same old ploy, no matter what one said.

'But I'm afraid one won't get the chance to do that,' I said. Just a remark like that is as good as an invitation. Don't you think? The play was in full swing. According to unchangeable, unspoken rules.

'My god, why do you have to be so down to earth?' he said.

'Why do you have to be so up in the clouds?'

'Do you know something? I like girls with brains. You know, Jeannette, the one I was supposed to meet tonight, you can't talk to her about anything. I mean anything serious. Are you coming home with me?'

'But I told you . . .'

70

'I know, I know. I heard what you said. I promise. Swear on the Bible.'

'Really? Do you believe in the Bible?'

'No.'

'Then you must swear by something else.'

'I swear. Honestly, I swear. I swear by myself.'

That was no doubt as good a thing as any to swear by. 'You're coming? I have a little moonshine. You can't say no to that, can you?'

'Now listen. If you think you're in the middle of the old play between a man and woman, you're wrong. It's nice talking to you. And I am lonely. My girlfriend's left me. If I come with you, that's the reason.' I spoke slowly, all the time looking into his eyes.

He put on a very serious face. The face of the law student. The frank and incorruptible eyes of the lawyer-to-be. He said, 'I've heard what you've said, and I'm prepared to talk to you, and nothing more.'

'No bed?'

'No bed.'

I believed him. As we were walking through the streets I felt rather at ease. He was tall and good-looking, and everyone must have thought I was his girl, and, as a matter of fact, I have never got over the sweetness of this kind of pride.

He lived on the fifth floor of the apartment building in Pilestredet, in a tiny, rectangular room facing the backyard, and he had a view of all the other tiny rectangular rooms opposite.

He took a bottle of bourbon out of his cupboard, but it didn't contain bourbon. His uncle was responsible for its contents – a grandiose uncle in Gudbrandsdalen who had just been to town. I took his moonshine on the rocks, though he warned me. It tasted like a slow flame. He sat beside me on the bed, there was hardly anywhere else to sit, but he got up at once and put on 'Zorba's Dance.' Then he stood in the

71

middle of the little floor, stretched out his arms and smiled and bowed his knees and was Anthony Quinn. He sat down beside me.

'I liked the film. Did you see it?'

'Yes, it was good.'

I felt his hand on my shoulder. Oh, I'd known it all along. What business did I have to believe that he would think I was a lesbian when I looked like a woman?

'Oh . . . please stop it,' I said.

'It doesn't matter, does it? My arm doesn't do any harm.'

'Yes, it does. What would you have said if a man had done that to you?'

'But I'm not a queer!' he exclaimed. A good explanation. That was it in a nutshell. 'I'm not a queer' is always a much better argument than to say that one is.

I tried to shake his hand off, but it only glided a little further down, and then it was there again. He started pulling me towards him. This was no longer funny. Why did I have to think that men had changed in the course of the last few months?

'Stop it!' I said.

'Just one kiss?'

'No, I won't. I told you I don't want men.'

'The men you have met must have been useless.'

He was getting wild and hot now. He forced me underneath him on the bed.

'Stop it!' I said, trying to get away. He held me tight, and pressed his mouth against mine. I pressed my lips together tightly. 'Stop it!' I shouted. He tried to force my lips open with his tongue and put his hand on my breast at the same time. Strategy.

'Stop it!' I shouted again. 'If you don't stop it, I'll be furious.'

I got up and looked for my duffel coat. He got up too and took me around the shoulders. I asked him to let go, and repeated that I would be furious, and said I wanted to leave. Leave? Now that we were having such a good time? He tried to hold me. Just one kiss. No, hadn't he heard what I said? What about his promise? Yes, but just one kiss. Didn't he understand that when I said no, I meant no? But didn't I like him? Yes, he was quite all right. I had my duffel coat on now. He barred my way. Why couldn't I stay? He took hold of me again, and pressed his hand between my legs. I got so furious that it hurt inside. At the same time I knew I had given him the resistance he wanted – so that his final conquest of me as a woman would be even sweeter. There was no way out of this. This was how thousands of women did it, without meaning it. Or was I wrong? Did they mean no but then just give in?

I pushed him away so ferociously that he stumbled backwards against the table in surprise, since he hadn't expected me to get so furious, and his bottle of moonshine overturned. I flung the door open, rushed out and ran down the long, empty corridor, hearing him swearing and shouting. I didn't wait for the lift, but ran all the way down the stairs, and didn't stop for a moment to see if he was coming until I was safely down in Pilestredet. The street was empty. The only person I saw was a man in a coat and tie. I hurried in the opposite direction.

Now you probably understand better what I meant when I said I do foolish things, though I think wisely about them. Any idiot would have known how this was going to end. My problem is that I won't accept it. I won't accept it till the end of time. Nevertheless, anyone would say that if I had been raped there, or even killed, it would have been my own fault.

You're looking a bit awkward. Aren't you comfortable? Shall I get you another cushion? You know, I want you to be comfortable as long as you're listening to my story. I didn't invite you home with me in order to make you awkward, you know. I invited you to make you wiser. Perhaps it isn't the right way to go about it. I don't know. Perhaps you're just waiting for me to finish. Perhaps you're not even listening.

Do you want some beer? You know, men often drink beer in literature, so there's nothing the matter with your having a beer now. Your mouth must be rather dry after having listened to so much talking.

There you are. Cheers! Have you heard the famous saying among men: 'If a lady says "No" she means "Perhaps", if she says "Perhaps", she means "Yes", and if she says "Yes", she isn't a lady'?

That's a good one, isn't it? That's a really good one. But how are we supposed to say 'No' and mean 'No'?

ELEVEN

The safe alibi

This was how my first attempt at breaking the isolation ended. But it wasn't to be my last attempt. After all, I'm a brave little soul.

Am I boasting? Perhaps you think so, but I'd like to mention one thing, in case you've forgotten. This was in the wonderful, radical year of 1968. The year that nowadays – for some obscure reason – has the reputation for being a time of student revolution, movements and protests throughout the European capitals. Including Oslo. The year that's given its name to a whole generation of radicals who wanted a better world. Well, I can tell you that the piece of news that aroused most attention among the students of Oslo that year was the news that Prince Harald, our king to be, was to marry Sonja – a commoner. Nothing whatsoever was discussed more eagerly than that. And what a good piece of news it was, too.

And in this year of student revolt and new ideas challenging the established order of things, there wasn't a single person in the whole of our kingdom who openly had declared himself a homosexual. Or herself. Nobody. The Finn Grodal I told you about earlier was still the only person one had ever heard named. And that was a pseudonym. Nobody even *talked* about homosexuals. Even though the University of Oslo was full of them. That was the state of affairs. I often wonder why people forget so easily. Since we've had this homo menace now for some years, people seem to think it was always so.

I'll tell you what happened at the University of Oslo in the glorious year of 1968. I knew by then that there must be several other perverts around, but where were they? I never saw anyone. I continued going to the club. I couldn't give up the hope of happiness. One day she would come. It sometimes happened that I sent long glances after someone or other, either because she had a fascinating voice or looked a little less stupid than the rest, but such women almost always belong to someone else.

So there I sat – alone with my beer and trying to look as though I wasn't sitting there alone with my beer at all, and wearing the expression of someone who wasn't looking for someone at all.

Most of the crowd were men, anyway. As we'd already seen on the first day. Then one night, when I was sitting there as usual, Ulrik came along. He confided in me that he was a student at the university at Blindern.* Hadn't he seen me there? Yes. He was the first person I'd met who admitted he was a student and a homosexual at the same time.

My God! Was there really a connection between the clandestine life within the walls of the club and the life led between lecture rooms with notes and *Paradise Lost* under my arm? In recent months I had more and more come to think of myself as having a split personality. When I was sitting in the cafeteria at Blindern looking at the ocean of coffee-drinking, determined faces, I thought, If only they knew where I spend my Saturday evenings! When I was on my way to our hiding-place, I thought, If only they knew that I'm going *there*.

But there, suddenly, was Ulrik. He stood there in front of me, smiling a confidential, boyish smile and looking to me

*Blindern is where the modern university campus of Oslo is situated.

76

like the most honest person I had ever seen. He knelt down by the side of my chair, and said, 'There must be many more of us at the university, don't you think? Hundreds? But where are they?'

This was the beginning of a very long friendship. We used to sit for hours in the evenings talking to each other about our lives. It was almost like being in love. And never was I safer with a man. And never was he safer with a woman.

The people around us immediately started acknowledging the connection. They invited us to all sorts of parties, taking it for granted that we were what we weren't. And we left them in the dark as best we could. We went hand in hand on Carl Johan, and we even discussed getting married. It was a time of untruthful bliss. Ulrik and I had found the safe alibi.

Then we got married and lived untruthfully ever after.

I can see from the shock on your face that you didn't expect my story to end like that. Well, it doesn't. As a matter of fact, we didn't marry at all. That was a lie just to impress you. Instead we decided to do something for all our fellow queers. We wrote a pamphlet saying that homosexual students ought to stop hiding themselves. But before we distributed it around the campus, we went to the university director himself and asked his permission. We were afraid of doing something illegal. And everything has to be very legal. Especially with us.

Ulrik was beside himself with nervousness as we sat there waiting outside the door. He was sure that the moment the director learned about our errand, he'd think that Ulrik had come to seduce him. Finally we were allowed to enter. The director was totally unprepared. Poor thing. He'd probably never seen homosexual human beings before – real live ones – but he tried to look as though he had. Yes, he said,

Mmmmm. And he listened to us, his hand under his chin. Well, if we really thought it was necessary . . . We did.

We handed out the pamphlets and gave an interview to *Dagbladet*. Everyone at the club thought it was marvellous. Very brave. Fancy going straight to the university director and saying you were a homosexual, and even saying something sensible afterwards. We became some kind of heroes. You should have seen their gratitude. Yes, I really wish you had. It proved, more than anything else, what the homosexual self-image was like.

Now, don't think that we'd done any of this openly. We didn't have our names in the paper, and we didn't hand out our pamphlets in the open, while people were sitting eating their cabbage rolls with six potatoes and parsley. No, we stayed anonymous and spread the pamphlets on tables and notice boards under cover of darkness, Ulrik in front with a cap pulled over half his face, I behind him with the hood of my duffel coat concealing everything but the tip of my nose, and the next morning we pretended that we didn't notice the pamphlets at all.

But for weeks, months and years later students at Blindern talked of the 'blue leaflets'. They had picked them up, glanced at them, and put them away in their pockets and bags immediately, and read them in safety when they got home to their digs.

At the club, Helen congratulated me. You remember Helen, the first woman I met there; the one who always wore a male suit and a tie? She said she would never in her life dare to tell anyone that she was a homophile.

TWELVE

For God so loved the world (John 3:16)

At about this time I met Kristin. Kristin was fulfilment. Also at about this time I met Nora. She'd picked up one of the blue leaflets and run with trembling hands to the lavatory to read it. Nora was not fulfilment.

I wasn't Nora's fulfilment either. She wrote to me under the name of 'Student group' to the post box number at Vika Post Office, Oslo central, and we met on a light spring evening outside the Valkyrien Restaurant. She was wearing a light blue spring coat and had obviously just been to the hairdresser. Later I realised that she always looked as if she'd just been to the hairdresser. We went in and ordered beer.

She insisted on paying, but she came into constant conflict with the waiter, who couldn't understand why we shouldn't pay separately.

She had read our message, and she thought I was courageous. It was the first time she'd told anyone she was a homosexual, and now she was forty-two years old. She had never had anything to do with men. In *that* way. She had never had anything to do with women either. In *that* way. But she had had a woman colleague whom she'd adored for years. She had been a secretary before she finally decided to become a student. That was really something she'd wanted to do for many years, and now she was studying French.

'I've just read *Le Mur* by Sartre,' she said. 'It's fantastic.'

'Yes,' I said, 'I can't help thinking of the man who took a woman up to his hotel room and sat down in a chair just to watch her undress. That's all he wanted.' I smiled foolishly. Perhaps I'd hit the wrong note. She laughed. But it was just a little tinkle in the throat, not a real belly laugh. This is sure to be a failure, I thought.

'Do you know what I think? I'm so against people assuming that homosexuals are just some sort of sexual beings . . .' she said.

'But aren't we? Why shouldn't we be allowed to be just as sexual as everybody else?'

She looked at me. There was something she wanted to explain. Now I shouldn't sit there and play the lesbian veteran for her. Let her say it. I couldn't help throwing a surreptitious glance at the big, curved breast under her light blue pullover while I pretended I was concentrating on my beer. She smiled a sweet smile at me. In her spare time she played the violin.

'I play the violin while I'm thinking of the woman I love, whom I can never have,' she said.

'Are you going to go on playing the violin?' I asked and smiled.

It was one of my more fortunate smiles this time. I was sure of that, since I was becoming a bit tipsy. Her hairstyle didn't bother me so much any more.

'I also write a few poems,' she said, and added cunningly, 'but perhaps you think I ought to stop that, too?'

'It depends what they're like.'

Whereupon she quoted one of her poems on the spot. There were flowers on the beach being washed away by the sea. I went home with her. She played 'In the Chapel in the Moonlight' for me on her violin and showed me her photo album – her brother with his bride, her sister with her bridegroom, her parents on their wedding day way back in

80

1920 and herself with a student cap – and she showed me some vases she'd made out of clay and then painted with little biblical motives.

She told me that when she was a young girl she had joined the Salvation Army hoping that her daily communion with Jesus and doing good works would make her forget her low desires. But what really happened was that she fell in love with the major. She did everything to please her and realised with terror that she thought more about this major than about anybody else, even Jesus – and when, moreover, she had to admit to herself that it gave her an exquisite transvestite thrill to wear a uniform, she went into a deep religious crisis.

She told me she had a secret dream. It was a dream she'd never dared to utter to any living soul. She dreamed that she was standing in front of the altar with the woman she loved and that she promised her to be true until death did them part. She got red in the face when she said it.

'It's a pact with God, you see,' she said. 'I talk to God every day.' (I wondered, Really? How is he getting on? I shut my mouth, however, in the very nick of time.) 'But there's something else. You know, I don't believe that God doesn't accept the love between two women, or between two men . . . Do you believe that?'

'I don't believe in God. I believed in him when I was a child. But he deceived me so many times I got tired of him. The God I know is evil. He doesn't even accept the love between man and woman. That's why he expelled them from paradise. Because he was jealous. He couldn't stand looking at them. If God sees everything, it must be a terrible fate, really. Jealousy sits in the eye, so he must have had a hell of a time. He had planned to have Adam all to himself, but then Adam moaned so for Eve that he had to make her. Didn't you know that God is a homophile?

'But didn't you say you don't believe in him?'

81

'I'm just talking about the God that I've heard of. He must be a homophile. I can't find any other explanation.'

'But to God jealousy and all ill-feeling are foreign. God is love.'

'Which God is that?'

'My God.'

'Oh. I've never heard about him. I've just heard about the God who explains all pain in this world with the words, This is my will.'

'But God's will is good.'

'How can evil be good?'

'It can. The will of God is always good, even if it may seem evil sometimes.'

'Very good.'

She laughed her mild tinkling laugh again, and again I had to glance a bit at her curved breast. But I failed completely in my attempt to say something that could make it move a bit.

'You're making a fool of me,' she said. 'I think that the Church has misunderstood. God himself sees that the love I have felt for the woman I love is a good love. The Church must finally come to realise that it has misunderstood God. And when it realises that, my dream will come true.'

Now I quivered with inward triumph. This was the ace of spades that I'd been waiting to beat with my small trump all through the cut and thrust of this conversation. Never had I met a more ideal combatant for my blasphemous thoughts.

'The Church has not misunderstood God. The Church has revealed God in all his wickedness. Therefore it will never accept homosexual couples. The Church must protect the evil of God, because if it doesn't, it will dissolve from within. Can't you see that?'

'No, I can't see that. God looks on us poor sinners with mercy, and the Church receives us. The Church will receive homosexuals one day, too.'

'As sinners, yes. "We accept the sinner, but not the sin,"

that's what they say. What does that mean? You must fear and love God, so that you don't accept homosexuality, but you do accept the homosexual. Funny, isn't it? But then, the Church is renowned for its sense of humour. The one about the Holy Ghost was also rather a good one.'

I knew I was mocking now, and I was going far beyond the limit. But Nora was a patient soul. I never got as close to seeing anyone with a halo as I did with her. I suppose she was a true Christian, as opposed to most people who go by that name. But anyway, why shouldn't I mock? The Church was mocking me. It mocks what I have of religious feeling, it mocks what's holy inside me. It mocks all women as long as it doesn't accept women priests. It mocks all homosexuals as long as it doesn't accept their true feelings. It encourages us to *lie* about ourselves. Because asking forgiveness for our love of someone of our own sex would be a *lie*. But that's what it asks us to kneel down and do. That's mockery.

But Nora was meek and mild. She said, 'I think that one day the Church will realise it's wrong, that it has been wrong all the time. Homosexuality is not a sin, and one day the Church will realise that there's a place for everyone in heaven. Even us.'

'Really? Why isn't there a place for Satan, then, in the kingdom of God? What makes you think you're so much better than Satan? Who but an evil power would say to me, "I condemn you to eternal suffering if you don't believe in me"? Isn't that the commandment of a wicked and vengeful figure thirsting for power? The Church has not misunderstood God. It has hit God's nail on the head. Caught him in the act of ambition. Our appeal to the Church to accept us is really an appeal to misinterpret God's message.'

'You're not very religious,' she said. For a moment I was at a loss for an answer. That was true. I'd never accepted authority. That's my real flaw, of course. I'd never accepted that people or institutions were *right*, just because of their position. But that's what you're supposed to accept from the very start. Why do people have to have an authority? They seem to need it. I'd never needed one.

'But the Christian faith is a religion of love,' she said.

'Do you think so? When did it become that? People go around thinking that the essence of the Christian message is: "Love thy neighbour!" But it's not true. The Christian message is: "For God so loved the world, that he gave his only begotten Son, that whosoever disbelieveth in him, should perish, and have everlasting pain." St John 3:16. Also called the little Bible.'

'Oh dear, you're preaching a blatant obscurantist religion!'

'I'm interpreting the obscurantist religion that I see.'

'Yes, but you didn't quote that passage cor–'

'Open your book and follow closely. How would you interpret it? Do you think we can abolish hell just because some liberal preachers pat us on the back and say we shouldn't be too worried about it?'

'But God's mercy! To me God's mercy is the most essential part of the faith, and the enormous generosity that the mercy springs from.'

'What are you going to do with the mercy? Can't you see it's meaningful only if we accept the core of Christian faith – that is, that there are two basic principles hovering about in the universe, the principle of good and the principle of evil. The principle of evil is black and has a vicious smile in the corner of its mouth. The principle of good is a small, light and friendly cloud-formation with a halo over it. Therefore some people must be debased and some must be exalted. Suffer the little homophiles to come unto me, hinder them not, for theirs is the kingdom of heaven. Hallelujah. What value is there in the kingdom of God if everybody gets there? But perhaps you think it would be all right if the Church stopped trampling on homosexuals and went on trampling on other people? The heavenly palace on high can only maintain

84

its glory when there are also the dark depths of hell.'

'I think hell is here on earth. I don't believe in a hell beyond. We have to abandon medieval dogmas. And the Church has great power over minds. It means a great deal to people that the Church condemns us. If we could make some liberal preachers stand up and bless homosexual love, many of the popular prejudices against us would vanish.'

'Do you really want to be used as a hostage to prove the liberal thinking of a few preachers? What interest do we have in making the Church more durable, as long as its basis is that every one of us is supposed to go around isolated from everyone else and feel sinful? As long as it expects us to accept that our individual sinfulness can be redeemed only through the death of another human being? The essence of the faith is not that you should love your neighbour as yourself; the essence is to love *God*. And that means to do his will, whatever it is. If it is his will to go and hang yourself on a cross, you should do that. God gave man free will to do his will. That's the freedom he offers you. Yes. If the little homophiles come creeping, they will surely partake of God's mercy.'

'I think you're twisting it.'

'Yes. That's just because you think that Christian belief is the peal of organs and Bach and church spires in the moonlight. It wasn't Bach's fault that the organs were placed in churches. I could also very well fancy a reflective hour with my beloved, but it has nothing to do with the Bible and Per Lönning.'*

As you can imagine, I was really in my element. I assumed that she was feeling less and less in hers. I had become pretty intoxicated. I always think that I'm saying the deepest truths then. Everything I say becomes so essential. Of course I don't remember just as clearly what she said, but my

*Per Lönning is one of the more liberal ministers in Norway. But even he has said that he believes homosexual feeling to be inferior to heterosexual.

85

my impression is that I won the discussion.

As you might have guessed, this was not the beginning of a great erotic experience. Any sparks that may have flown between us in the heat of battle can be left untold. We did not go to bed with each other. It's disappointing, I know. But you see, it does happen, just once in a blue moon, that two lesbians who are alone together don't go to bed with each other, but sit talking instead. This was one such occasion. We got up from our chairs, looked out of the window, and there we saw it – a full, blue moon, rising above the tree-tops.

THIRTEEN

Arise, you homos from your slumbers*

Well. That's how my first attempt at breaking the isolation of my fellow lesbian sisters ended. While Ulrik was having a rush of excited young male students coming to see him as a result of the blue leaflets, and had a great time for months introducing them to gay life, I had only this one biblical battle.

Yet it was a successful one, as it turned out. She did the rest herself. When I met her at the club some months later, she'd cut her hair short and was wearing a red waistcoat and stiff collar and walked with long steps between the tables, shouting, 'Hey, folks!' Before long she was indistinguishable from those with cigars and hormones, and one would never have suspected her of ever having seen a lady's hairdresser. Whether the transformation extended to the depths of her faith in the will of God, I don't know, but I doubt it.

Now you may have forgotten about Kristin. But I haven't. You know, when something is really important, one usually just brushes it aside, and behaves as if nothing has happened. One must take care not to give the impression that something that means something, means something.

*From the international workers' song 'Arise, you workers from your slumbers', commonly sung at 1 May celebrations, a national holiday in Norway.

I have a rather warped attitude towards sex. I never really know whether I can be bothered to engage in it or not – in the long run. I think sexual intercourse is a pretty exhausting performance that often doesn't live up to one's expectations. Since it's a matter of life and death whether it leads to an orgasm or not, it often doesn't. One is so obsessed by the thought of its leading to orgasm that the orgasm doesn't come.

Now they pop up again. The researchers with the theories. They come hovering through the air. A number of male characters. With blueprints of the orgasm in their briefcases.

Orgasm is a physiological phenomenon. Now, we'll tell you something rather remarkable. A woman is also equipped with a kind of thingumy-bob that in a way may be described as a penis. Everyone heaves a sigh of relief. Have we really? Then perhaps we aren't completely good for nothing, after all? We're almost moved to tears by the suggestion. Just think of it – a kind of penis! Oh, lucky, lucky me!

We call it a clitoris. We smile a nice smile and draw a clitoris on the blackboard. We're living in modern times – so we do that. An example of a fine specimen in a state of high excitation twenty times enlarged. The almost-penis of woman.

'When thith ith thimulated, dear children, for a thufficient period of time, and rhythmically – remember that! – the woman getth what ith called an orgathm. It ith exthremely important for the woman to get her thatithfaction through the orgathm.'

Orgasm in the conjugal bed, orgasm on the bus, orgasm in the open and orgasm at home, orgasm in your heart, orgasm in your mind – orgasm, only orgasm. To be sung to the tune of 'Old Folks at Home'. The fact that some lyrics don't fit with the tune has never prevented any Norwegian from singing a song. Every bird pipes its own lay. Every bird moans its own orgasm.

Oh, hot-blooded woman who screams with joy at my touch – lie down and be Anna Magnani to me, before we sneak along with our briefcases to the next audience.

Orgasm is a point from whose source all things radiate and sparkling rainbows and wild flowers are revealed in multi-coloured splendour, and you discover that you don't love the one you went to bed with, after all.

This is where Kristin comes in. Because I loved her. And I had orgasms with her, too. But I won't tell you about the flowers I saw. Only that they were yellow and violet and whirled around like a scent from a childhood dream.

I didn't meet her in a bar in Casablanca. I did tell you, didn't I, that one doesn't necessarily meet one's lesbian true love there? Nor did I meet her at our homophile meeting-place at the clandestine rowing club down the alley. I didn't meet her by distributing those blue leaflets at the university campus, either. In fact, I met her in a queue.

It was one of those queues that were always common at the beginning of term, when one has to queue up for every little thing that has to be put straight before you can plunge into your books. Queues for your student identification card, queues to have chest X-rays, queues to register for seminars, queues just for the hell of queuing up. We had been standing in one of those queues in the September heat for quite a long time; it hardly seemed to move, when the person in front of me whose back I'd been watching for ages suddenly turned around and said, 'What are we actually waiting for?' She looked into my eyes enquiringly and didn't stop looking.

'I don't know,' I said, because in fact I didn't. I was just standing there to be sure I didn't miss whatever it was. It turned out that none of the others knew why we were standing there either.

We went to the campus cafeteria – a cosy 300 square yard hall – and queued up for a cup of coffee instead. It was there, in the middle of the smell coming from the huge pans of cabbage rolls, mashed spuds and gravy that I first started to feel that strange, unmistakable emotion that I'm supposed to be ashamed of. As we gathered round the table – there were about seven of us who'd given up on the queue – Kristin talked astonishingly, entertaining all of us with her wit. She said, 'I'm a lesbian. How about you? Are you lesbian, too? How do you know, if you think you aren't?' Most of the students round the table laughed in bewilderment, and I think we were all uncertain whether she really meant it. 'It's stupid,' she continued, 'to go around hiding, just because of a few feelings.' The others nodded. They all agreed. Very stupid. 'Some time ago I picked up one of those blue leaflets lying around here,' Kristin went on. 'I wonder who on earth had the guts to put them out. Did you see those blue leaflets?' Everybody nodded. They'd all seen the blue leaflets. But she looked at me, since I just sat there moping inwardly. 'B . . . blue leaflets?' I muttered. Kristin started eagerly to explain what they had said.

Later I met her accidentally quite a number of times, and we had coffee. She told me quite openly about her feelings and frustrations, and how she'd finally seen the light. But having started with a lie, I never got round to saying anything about mine. I was gradually and very noticeably falling in love with her.

Then she phoned. I recognised her voice immediately, but I'd never given her my phone number, and I doubt if she knew my surname. She was talking quickly, as if she were out of breath, stammering and hesitating. I'd never heard her like that before, and I soon realised she didn't know whom she was talking to. She stammered that she'd got my phone number through the post box in Vika, because I was in that homophile student group in the Society of 1948. Could I meet her?

We agreed that we would meet at the corner of Josephine Street and Pilestredet.

That's how Kristin came into my life, riding on a white horse to win the victory. Actually, she came riding on a black bicycle, and there was a thunderstorm. She came five minutes too late, turning up on the other side of the street, braking with her right leg on the pavement. I went across to her, trying to pretend that nothing in the world concerned me. She looked at me with the eyes that at that moment I knew I loved. The weather was hot and damp. Her hair was falling into her face; she blew it away, only to make it lift a bit and fall back. 'What are you doing here?' she said. 'You see, I was going to meet somebody . . .' She looked around. A woman who looked like a secretary was coming up the street. We both stared at her. But she didn't stare back. She went past. 'That wasn't her,' Kristin said. 'No,' I said, 'no wonder.' 'No wonder?' 'Yes,' I said, 'because it's me.' 'You?' 'Yes. You're meeting me.' 'I can see that, but . . .' She turned towards me, 'You mean to say, *you're* the one I'm supposed to meet?' 'Yes.'

She started laughing. She started an uproarious and insane laugh, a laugh that echoed through all the surrounding houses, she laughed her hair into confusion, and then she turned to me very solemnly and said, 'What a laugh!'

Lightning flashed. 'Isn't it wonderful?' she said. 'Yes,' I said, not knowing whether she meant the weather or me. 'I don't like sunny weather,' she said, 'it reminds me of all the things I didn't do'.

We started walking along the wall of the Bislet Stadium. For the first time since we'd met, we said nothing. We went up past the pre-war buildings in Collets Street and came to the crossing at Ullevålsveien. We stopped. Where were we going? She'd thought I lived somewhere in the neighbourhood. I'd thought she lived here. We looked foolishly at each other. Then we went up to the hill of Saint Hans. It must have been instinct that drew us to this place – a beautiful green hill in the middle of our murky town. The ancient spark had arisen again. The grass was wet.

'I've been beside myself all day,' she said. 'I was so nervous about calling you.'

'Didn't you recognise my voice?'

'No. I hardly heard my own.'

This was a new Kristin. I'd never thought her capable of nerves. Now she said she was deeply depressed, and that she'd bought half a bottle of brandy. That's why she was late. I was falling more and more in love with each step. By the time we reached the top of the hill, the whole of me was a jelly of happiness.

We found a secluded spot in the beautiful, green grass. There she got out the half bottle of brandy from her bike bag and we each took a gulp. It was like an act of confidence. At least to me.

'Actually, I've seen you before,' she said. 'I mean, before we met in the queue.'

'Where?'

'In the Oslo Women's Society.* Sometimes.'

'Did you go there, too?'

'Yes, but in a way I felt like an outsider. What they said fascinated me. But I felt my presence there wasn't justified. All they said had to do with women's direct relationship to men. Doing housework and being allowed to take a job outside the home. Lesbians were never mentioned, and if they had been, it would have been a shock. It was as if the oppression of lesbians had nothing to do with the women's cause. I felt that my lesbianism would be seen as a liability to feminism.'

This was exactly what I'd felt myself. There was no link between homosexuality and feminism, and I was glad, too, that nobody there knew I was a lesbian.

*Norsk Kvinnesaksfovening, the first feminist organisation in Norway founded in 1884.

92

'Actually, I knew you were a lesbian the moment I saw you,' Kristin said.

I was shocked. I'd always been grateful that I didn't look as though I was about to move the grand piano. I took another gulp from the bottle. The view over the town was beautiful from here. The green hill stretched out in front of us with small, round white flowers on it. I felt her exquisitely near. Especially along my right upper arm. There was a space of about half an inch between my arm and hers, and in this space a number of invisible minute pulses were busy sparking to and fro with incessant energy. I moved over to pick one of those small white flowers just in front of her left shoe, pressing my arm against hers in doing so. That's how I always do it in situations like this. Now you know. That's how we do it.

I don't want you to believe that I'm easily spurred on. Like that. But I am.

I get easily excited, if you really want to know. And quickly. And I don't believe that the love I feel is as superior as the love most other people feel. For instance, priests.

It was then that this sort of inferior feeling that I know started to develop for the person sitting beside me on the grass. It was a long time now since I'd felt it. I knew at once. I hadn't had these feelings since my friendship with Tove. But for her I had had some really strong, inferior feelings, and it was wonderful to feel that they were now coming back.

Kristin told me she had just broken an engagement with a medical student. They had been to a psychologist, who had suggested aversion therapy, but the medical student didn't believe in aversion therapy. He believed in reward therapy instead. But he was not rewarded.

There was something about Kristin that made me feel I had always known her. I liked her face. Oh, yes – I liked her face. You know? Does it happen that you sometimes like someone's face like that? Well, anyway, I burst into sharing confidences with her, telling her the story of my normal romance, too. Because, you see, once upon a time I had also been with a male.

His name was Robert, and he loved me. He did all the things I wanted, and if I had said I wanted the moon, he would have brought it down to me. We went to London and Paris together, we strolled along the banks of the Seine, went up the stairs to Sacré Coeur and lit a candle, traversed the Louvre, stopping in front of the Mona Lisa and making an ingenious plan to steal her – we always made up stories in the middle of the story we were actually in – and in the end we would go to live in a windmill in Holland. It was perfect. The only thing was, I wasn't in love with him.

On our way home we went through Hamburg, and there – in the so-called quarters of joy and entertainment in the district of St Pauli – we stopped in front of a bookshop. In the window there was a title in black that immediately rushed to my eye: *Die Homosexualität der Frau*.* It was a thick book and it cost DM 35. This was the moon. I knew that this was the one moon impossible for him to bring down to me. He paid for everything. But I knew I couldn't ask him for this. So while standing there I thought, 'I'm coming back here. I'm coming back here alone to buy that book.'

But I didn't. I didn't have the money and I wouldn't have known my way back there, anyway. But the title with its black letters remained in my brain. This thick book was the only concrete proof I had seen in the world that there was such a thing as love between women. I was not alone.

Kristin laughed a bit sadly.

'Why do we try for so long, when we know it's no use?'

'But we don't really know. We go on hoping and praying that we're normal.'

'Did you? I didn't. It's a matter of choice. After all, one

*Female homosexuality. [Translator's note]

94

isn't born a lesbian.'

'I was.'

'Well, I wasn't. And I don't think anyone is. Or did you fall in love with the midwife?'

'Yes.'

We stared into mid-air thinking of the deep truth of the last statement. There were a few scattered raindrops. The sky looked threatening. There was thunder some distance away.

'In a moment it's going to pour. That will be marvellous. I love rain.'

It pelted. It splashed down on our heads, down inside our collars, the ground became soaked under us, little creeks ran down the hill. She poured some cognac into one of them and drank. Then we took off our shoes and drank from them making a crook of our arms like they did in *Ben Hur*. Then we started to roll down the hill and laugh. We went up again and embraced to make a perfect wheel and rolled down the hill once more like we did when we were five, laughing and throwing our shoes up in the air, and we started to sing:

Arise, you homos from your slumbers
Arise from falsehood dark and sly!

We supplied each other with terrific suggestions for our protest song. Third line:

Stop hiding from your dear old auntie.

But that didn't rhyme with 'slumbers'. It ought to rhyme, but it didn't. How about: 'Stop hiding from your dear old family'? No, that wasn't much better. Now, listen to this:

Don't hide yourself in woods and lumbers
For you must honour mum and dad!

No, that's too rude. And 'dad' doesn't rhyme with 'sly', though one could change 'sly' to 'sad', of course. But we don't want a sad song, we want a bold and brave anthem. Pomp and Circumstance. Fourth line:

Give all who ask a true reply.

Too boring? How about: 'Come out and show your ass nearby'? No, that won't do. It will only reinforce people in their prejudices. We can keep the one with 'true reply'. It's true enough. Fifth line:

Let the Bible's preachings slowly perish

No, no – then people will only shy away from us. We must pretend that we think the Bible is all right. Kristin thought intensely for a while. Then she raised her finger and howled, 'I've got it!'

Join the chorus of the ones who dare blurt
Taboo word out true and bare:
'Hey, I'm a homosexual pervert!
And if you wish, just stop and stare!'

Bam-bam-bam-bam. That's the drums. Then comes the chorus: 'Then we'll meet down at the Queer Club!' No, no. That's precisely what we won't do. A new time is a-coming. We're coming out of the closet. Yes, aren't we? 'Then we'll meet in parks and alleys.' No, no. Nobody is supposed to know about that.

Then we'll meet along the high road
Coming out in numbers grand

That sounds like a national anthem. That's how we want it to sound. Something with appeal for the masses. Powerful and moving. Last two lines:

> Enough to shake the hetero code
> Throughout the fatherland!

Repeated:

> Enough to shake the heterosexual code
> Throughout our fatherland!

Kristin soon found pencil and paper and noted down our piece of poetry, which we roared through with gusto and vigour.

Of course, we assumed that the song would quickly slide into the compulsory curriculum of every schoolbook in the country. Young poetry. When we came to the fatherland bit, we were pretty intoxicated.

Then we suddenly saw a lady with an umbrella, trudging through the rain. We quickly climbed up into two trees nearby and hid.

'Cuckoo, cuckoo!' I cuckooed.

'Ho-moo, ho-moo!' Kristin cuckooed back.

The umbrella stopped.

'Did you hear the cuckoo?' I called encouragingly. The lady's face appeared and glanced up into the air.

Kristin waved a branch. 'Cuckoo,' I clamoured. 'Now you can make a wish come true!'

'But you shouldn't tell a single soul.'

The lady had caught sight of us. The corners of her mouth moved slightly. Kristin and I nearly fell out of trees, our arm muscles were getting so weak.

'Hello, down there!' Kristin shouted and waved her hand in the best prime-ministerial fashion. 'We're homosexuals!'

'Yes', I added and let my nicest Colgate smile shine

through the foliage. The lady started trudging again. Some steps later she stopped and turned around.

'Well, so am I,' she said, 'but I still don't behave like a cuckoo.'

Then she went away. We climbed down, succumbing to increasing fits of laughter, and embraced on the grass mat.

I'm telling you about this episode on the hill of Saint Hans mainly because I think it's important that you don't think there is anything peculiar about homosexual women. We're ordinary common people, who behave averagely. A homosexual woman is like any man in the street.

We had sexual intercourse on the spot. Half naked, while the September rains were pouring down on our overheated bodies. That's how we do it. Plain and simple.

Two days later we moved into a two-roomed flat in one of the suburbs.

FOURTEEN

What's what

Nobody celebrated. Family and friends did not come with tears in their eyes throwing rice as we crossed the threshold, nor did anyone give us silver spoons, knives and forks or a precious old vase. Don't think I'm not bitter because of this. No. It's a constant source of bitterness to me, so whenever I can't think of anything else to make me bitter, I think of this. I'm very greedy, you know. Very greedy.

So we moved in in secluded bliss. On the threshold, of course, we had an argument about who was going to carry whom across it. This was, as you can see, a variant on the dildo confusion, and we solved it by embracing and lying down and *rolling* into the hall. In this way one might say we carried each other into our new home. Necessity is the mother of invention.

Then we lay on the same hall floor for a week, making love. It was a marvellous time.

We did not, however, keep ourselves to ourselves for very long. Kristin was not one for disguising her homosexual propensities. We went hand in hand in the streets and did our best to make everyone see how happy we were. They saw it, too, because during this time we were so gloriously happy that nobody could miss noticing it. We beamed. At each other and at the world. The world looked back in confusion or looked away. In daylight, that is. At night, its real reactions came stealing back. After a while we could divide men in restaurants into four categories. First, there were the ones who pretended not to notice us, or actually didn't. (Were they homosexual, I wonder?) Then there were those who talked to us and went away the moment we said we weren't interested in making friends. This was a terribly small group, who must probably suffer from some minority problems. Thirdly, there were the men who settled down at our table. The more we bombarded them with sarcasm and refusals, the more comfortably they settled down. They assured us that they thought it was quite all right between two women, and that it was foolish that so many people were prejudiced against it, but two men, that was appalling. Quite abominable. They assured us about seventeen times how appalling and abominable they thought it was, thus making us understand how extremely heterosexual they were themselves. And potent. This category of men used to allow their flow of words to end up in a proposal to come home with us and watch. Just watch. No matter what price we asked.

I think your eyes are flickering. Are you recognising this category by any chance? I promise I'll release you from your awkward position soon. This moral lecture wasn't exactly what you'd expected, I know. But I promise I won't keep you much longer.

The fourth category resembled the third, in the sense that sarcastic remarks and jokes at their expense didn't move them from their post. On the contrary, they took them to be a titillating invitation. Two nice girls like us couldn't be lesbians. No, lesbians were ugly, unattractive women who looked exactly like men. Do you find men so ugly then? we asked. To which they would answer 'Yes' or 'Looks don't count with men' or 'Men are men' or something like that, but we were certainly not lesbians. The moral was: if we would only go to bed with them – because they all had a really big thing – then they'd show us what's what.

The ones who knew what's what were the most difficult to get rid of.

Now you mustn't think that we were sitting in those restaurants hugging and kissing and 'provoking', as it's called when we do things openly that other young lovers do all the time. No. We were sitting there talking quite nicely like good girls. But they sensed it, nevertheless. It was the ubiquitously penetrating lesbian spark.

Since none of these men got their way with us, in the end they had to look down into the abyss of truth. We were lesbians. When the men of categories three and four realise this, they stare into a complete void. They stare at an unknown realm of human activity into which they are not admitted. This is a horrifying experience. Since they were little boys they've been told that their activities are wanted everywhere and that the essence of womankind is to wait for the glory of their tools. So, confronting this new chance of getting to know the variety of the world, they repudiate it. They won't see what they see. They won't accept that they are not wanted. They suddenly become like little boys who stamp their feet and scream in desperation to get the ice-cream they were promised. But when this doesn't help, they have only one possibility left: they start using their brains.

This, of course, can sometimes be a promising pastime, leading to glorious results. But not in this case. They start using their brains to form theories that fit into their universe, not theories to expand it.

One of these theories is the titillation theory. It says that women are lesbians in order to titillate and excite men sexually. The titillation theory finds its home in category number three. The second theory is the bee-in-our-bonnets theory. This theory is rather touching. According to this theory, lesbianism is a kind of bee in one's bonnet, a caprice or a whim, a kind of escape from the real thing, a pastime while one is waiting for something better: a man. This theory is held by the fourth category.

When the third and fourth categories discover that neither of these theories holds water, they make up a third theory saying that we're lesbians because we've never met a Real Man. According to the Real Man theory, all the males we have met have been impotent. We have been walking through life for all of twenty-three years, but we have never come across anything except impotent members of the other sex.

It's curious how they can imagine this to be so. They can't have a very high opinion of other members of their own sex. At the same time, *they* excel in it and are prouder of being males than of anything else. The conclusion can only be that every man thinks his own potency is greater than that of everybody else.

But when or if the third and fourth categories of men discover that all these theories are false, they launch into a fourth theory with great inventiveness to cover up their fiasco: the big, crushing and final aversion theory. This theory is very logical. It says that when we aren't lesbians because we want to excite men sexually, or because we're killing time waiting for a man, or because we've never met a real male, then the reason must be that we despise man, with all his equipment, all his works, and all his being. Perverse and distorted hatred of men, they conclude. The final verdict has been brought in. Their pride is preserved. I'm all right, thank you. *Goodbye*.

Then, finally, they leave. But not without muttering a flow of words saying how ugly we look and what dreadful clothes we've got on. Half an hour earlier we were the nicest and most good-looking girls about town.

Well, such was our married bliss. Whom could we turn to? Who would rejoice in the happiness that we really felt? What should we do in order to prevent it from going stale? Who

102

could help but lesbians themselves?

We're accused of crowding into ghettos. Can't you see we had no choice but to go there? Nowhere else was there a place possible for our feelings. Nowhere else did we find mirrors of our own selves. And without that, it's hard to survive.

Margaret Mead has said, 'No personality is strong enough to survive fully in a society where it is threatened by the loss of sex membership.' I think that's true. So we had to make up such a community ourselves. That's the lesbian movement. But the difference between the lesbian movement and the ghetto is that we did it to come out – together – and offer that anarchist, feminist threat necessary for the expansion of the stale, male universe.

Because all those theories that we met coming out as a lesbian couple do not only concern us as lesbians. They concern all women since they show that men don't accept women as independent human beings. A woman is an appendix to a man. She always wants him. She has no business doing anything on her own. The clearest proof of this attitude is the male reaction to women doing *it* on their own. That's when their exasperation at female freedom rises to its peak. This exasperation hasn't got anything to do with sexual excitement at all. It has to do with the loss of power. To lose power is always frightening. Therefore lesbians are frightening to men. And we will remain so, whether we want to or not – whether we are bourgeois lesbians trying to live normal, hetero-copying lives, or lesbians joining the women's movement and demanding justice and a fair deal – as long as men won't give up their power position. And you can stop telling me that means we want all the women in the world to become lesbians. That hasn't got anything to do with it. It's sublimely irrelevant. The fear of lesbians is the fear of independent women.

FIFTEEN

Splashes from the wave of tolerance

I can see you're yawning. After all, it's about the only thing you can do in protest against my tale, firmly tied to your chair as you are. But like Ulysses passing the Sirens and tied to the mast of his ship, you agreed to being tied up as long as you were rewarded by learning how lesbians do it. It was your own suggestion, since we didn't trust you not to wander off. So we invited you home, thinking you must be an authentic specimen of humanity after all, since you were willing to go into voluntary confinement to learn the truth. I admit we were perfectly aware that this wasn't what you expected. But what's the point of experience if one only learns what one already knew?

Still, you must believe me when I say I'm sorry I put you in this position. But you asked for it. You wanted to know why the hell lesbians are lesbians, and I've tried to tell you. Lesbians are just lesbians. I've taken care to have a tape-recorder on all the time, so that I can tip it all down on to my typewriter later for the good of humanity. I could have given you this book to read, of course, when it's published, but I doubt if you would ever have read it. Men don't normally read what women write. Especially if it's about the absurdity and injustice that we have to suffer. Women read what women write. And they read what men write, too, and they sympathise and shed tears of compassion over men's frustrations and absurdities. So when I met you in that restaurant this evening, I could think of no other method of getting this message through to you.

Of course, when I release you from your ropes, you could go to the police and say you've been unlawfully tied up and kept prisoner in a lesbian's house, because she wanted to tell you how lesbians do it. But they'd probably laugh their heads off and say it was wishful thinking.

Anyway, I hope you won't do that. I hope you'll leave a wiser and better man, as the saying goes. Now I've almost finished my story. If you can call it that.

That winter Kristin and I got in touch with a liberal fellow in the student world. He was the editor of a leftist student paper, and he wanted to do an interview with some real lesbians. His motivation was, he said, that he was interested in the fate of social losers. I immediately started feeling I had lost an awful lot all my life and that I was a miserable and pitiable human creature.

He came home to our flat. Kristin disappeared, because she didn't want to be interviewed. I, on the contrary, at once started to feel very interesting and important because somebody found it worthwhile interviewing me. We had a pleasant talk during which I told him I was a homosexual, had always been a homosexual, and would probably go on being a homosexual for the rest of my life. He eagerly made notes on his pad.

As you probably realise, this man from the student world represented a new phase. Only the most suspicious of minds could attribute to him any of the four super-theories. He was much more advanced.

With a friendly smile he listened to all I said, and because he was such a pleasant character, I became more and more moved by my own statements.

I told him, and I'm telling you now, that the real burden of being a homosexual – or a lesbian if you wish – is that it forces you into dishonesty. It was not because of some political consciousness of a better world, or some belief in anarchism, feminism or a communist revolution, that I finally came out as a lesbian. It was because I couldn't stand lying.

I don't want to bring up the subject of homosexuality in every conversation I engage in. But if I don't *say* that I'm a homosexual, everyone naturally takes me for a heterosexual, so I have to say it. But when I say it, they can't take it naturally. And then the conversation turns into a conversation about homosexuality.

Try to imagine that you lived in a place where everyone took it for granted that you were a mason. But they didn't say it directly. It was just lying underneath everything that was said to you. And all the people you met also seemed to be masons and they went about building brick walls everywhere and thought it was very constructive and that all this masonry was just part of the natural state of affairs in the world. They never asked you, 'Are you a mason, too?' They asked, 'What kind of mixing spade do you prefer?' or 'Do you use red bricks or yellow bricks when you build houses?' And when you finally broke down and confessed to one of the masons that you weren't a mason at all, you were a carpenter, he looked completely crushed and said no more, but went home and read a book about carpenters in secret.

You saw this mason every day, but he didn't betray to any other human being that you were a carpenter. He was a reliable person. But three months later, when you were out one evening drinking beer at a pub together, just the two of you, and he'd had a pint too many, he started telling you that he'd thought a lot about *that*, and he'd read a book about *it*, and he'd come to the conclusion that it was wrong to look down on people who were like *that*. They couldn't help being carpenters (he lowered his voice at this word and looked surreptitiously about him) and preferring woodwork to brickwork. Woodwork could be rather beautiful, too, when one came to think of it. And then he assured you that he thought you were a swell guy all the same. He even got rather drunk and sentimental and said that perhaps there is a carpenter in every one of us. And when he got even drunker, he put his arm confidentially around your shoulders and said that he had done carpentry once as a small boy of twelve. Later he never referred to this conversation with you, but you were deeply grateful to him. He was among those people who tolerate carpenters.

I told this little allegory to my interviewer, and I quoted George Eliot's *The Mill on the Floss*, where she makes Maggie Tulliver say, 'It is other people's wrong feelings that make concealment necessary.' There must be something fundamentally wrong with a society where people are so afraid of feelings that they don't dare to speak about them.

Because that is the trouble. People don't speak about heterosexual feelings either. If you go home and say, 'I'm getting married', that's just accepted. But it doesn't mean talking about your feelings. It doesn't mean that you have to explain how you make love, or when on earth you realised that you wanted to marry, or what your precise feelings are for this man. Celebrating weddings isn't talking about feelings. It is just accepting a convention. But if you go home and say, 'I'm moving into a flat with my girlfriend and we are lovers', that's talking about feelings – even though you haven't implied any more than 'I'm getting married' implies.

So whatever you think about the present social order, you go against it by living the life that is natural to you and being honest about it – and that proves that there is something wrong with that order. Homosexual love is an act of anarchy. Though it ought not to be. It ought not to be anything in particular at all. Love is love.

That's how I came to realise that I don't want the

acceptance of this world. Not because I don't want to be accepted, because I do, but because it would be an acceptance by a world that denies truth.

Yes, I told you this was going to be a moral lecture, and that's what I gave my interviewer, too. He went happily home to his paper, but that he had become neither a better nor a wiser man was soon clear.

He produced a big headline. He assured his readers that I looked like a pleasant and normal girl, and that I spoke frankly and told him about my life with warmth and honesty. My appearance was that of a womanly woman, so you could read between the lines that I didn't look as though I was on my way to start the truck, and about to fix the carburettor and the drive shaft first.

As you can see, my interviewer was sailing on the big, new tolerance wave, where the following basic thought could be traced: 'Dear reader, *there is no reason to discriminate against them, because they're just like everybody else.* They fit into the pattern, dear reader, so don't you worry!'

Like other people who concern themselves scientifically with homosexuality, my interviewer had been very interested in prying into my past. I'd told him that I'd been a homosexual for as long as I could remember, and I could remember from the time I was three. (I didn't tell him about my infatuation for the midwife, since I guessed he wouldn't believe me.) Here the other basic thought appeared. 'Dear readers, *there is no reason to discriminate against them, because their homosexuality is no fault of their own.* They commit their acts in innocence, dear reader, and therefore they ought to be acquitted.' This implied that if there were people who actually chose to be homosexual, there should be no mercy.

My interviewer went on digging into my past. You must have been terribly unhappy, don't you think? When you were young, and saw all the others passing by in loving couples, whereas you had to hide your feelings? Tell me all about it. Yes. Just cry a bit. No wonder you're crying, thinking about those dreadful years. The time of youth, that ought to be such a beautiful and happy time, was for you a nightmare.

I must admit that I automatically crept into the fold of this sympathy. After all, how many people had I met who wanted to listen to my story? Of course I was unhappy when I was young. But who isn't? And my reasons for being unhappy weren't that I was in love, but that I couldn't say anything about it. Most young people have emotions that they don't dare to speak about. I was probably only as unhappy as everybody else. And after all, my close friendship with other girls, and my falling in love with some of them, made my life worth living. Often I thought, I'm luckier than a boy unhappily in love with a girl. I can be with the girl I love all the time.

Nevertheless, with this first experience of sympathy from the outside world, I plunged into self-pity, and was partly responsible for the result myself. It was: '*There is no reason to discriminate against them, because they are so unhappy.*'

But my interviewer also wanted to see the brighter side of life. Today I had found myself as a lesbian, and I had found another lesbian to live with, so today I had ended in the married bliss that I had always dreamed of. Then came the fourth and final and most alluring conclusion: '*There is no reason to discriminate against them, because today they are living happily together, two by two, in married bliss.*'

The relationship between Kristin and me, though he hadn't seen much of it, was described in terms of a perfectly normal relationship between husband and wife. We kissed each other when we parted, and we had a normal little flat, which was described in all its normal details – pictures on the walls, furniture, radio and records, toothbrushes, electric light bulbs, and water coming from the tap. There was no trace of deviation anywhere. The description reached its climax at the centre of all human joy: the conjugal bed. He also found out that Kristin was much better than I was at cooking.

We can give a sigh of relief. The most comfortable of all conclusions was at hand: '*There is no reason to discriminate against them, because they represent no threat to our way of life. No threat to the values of our present social order.* Dear reader, open your arms, and embrace them.'

Later I wondered what he'd expected, since he pointed to our perfect normality so often. Had he expected me to creep around on the floor on all fours with a wedding cake on my head, murmuring abracadabra, when Kristin went away, and to explain to him that this was the homophile parting ceremony?

Yes. The leftist man from the student world was an instructive acquaintance. He convinced me that there is one type of homosexual suitable for public presentation. The nice homo-type that we can all sympathise with. A bit helpless, perhaps. Or well-bred and articulate. But decidedly nice.

My interviewer did not for one moment deviate from the norm of presenting nice people to nice people. He behaved quite naturally. Almost like a normal person, I would say. There wasn't anything peculiar about him at all. During the interview he didn't once suddenly spring to his feet and say 'Moo'. And he probably lived happily with his nice newspaper for ever after.

SIXTEEN

A natural farewell

Do you think I'm unfair? He did his best, no doubt, and I never seem to be content. That's true. For what's the point of saying to the world: homosexuals are no threat? What's wrong with threatening a world that is threatened by death and starvation, overpopulation, oppression of peoples and alienation between women and men? I'm just asking. There must be a change. You know that as well as I do. But you don't make a change by forcing men and women to live together when they don't want to. You can shout, 'That's natural!' till you're dumb and blind, but it won't help. What's natural about living in secluded boxes? It's not natural for heteros, and it isn't natural for homos, either.

It's natural to beget children, you say. That's your trump card. But there's nothing wrong with our genitals, you know. Did you think so? We can have children if we want to, and we do. You don't have to live in nuclear families to beget children and bring them up. But a child must have a father and mother around, you argue. All right. Go and tell that to all the fathers who planted their seeds here there and everywhere. And then went away. What's wrong with mothers? A child needs love and care, that's what a child needs, and it doesn't come out of the womb saying it needs anything but a nipple. And warmth and a safe place to sleep. It has no preconceived ideas of what safety, love and care are going to look like. They can look like many things. You're talking about what's 'natural' as if it were a constant factor in human civilisation, and if you hear that human culture varies through all the ages and societies on earth, you turn to the animals. Oh, you don't know anything about animals? They aren't as heterosexual as you think.

Go out and watch the world around you. See the variety, just like Adam did. You need a new genesis.

Now I'll release you. Kristin and a number of other women who've been called here for the occasion are in the other room, mind you. Actually, they're sitting on the conjugal bed playing bridge. Culbertson's system. It's just in case you should try and rape me or commit some other kind of folly before you go. One never knows. I sincerely hope you've enjoyed this voyage through my lesbian odyssey. Goodbye.

Lillian Faderman
Surpassing the Love of Men

Romantic Friendship and Love between
Women from the Renaissance to the Present

'A fascination from beginning to end . . . a sort of
revelation'
Jill Tweedie, *The Guardian*

A quietly revolutionary book which reconstructs a lost history
of women loving women. Here Lillian Faderman explores the
different forms that love has taken over the years, from the
elaborate deceptions practised by Deborah Sampson, soldier of
the American Revolution, to the genteel Ladies of Llangollen
and the notorious 'Boston marriages' of the nineteenth
century.

Dr Faderman is a full professor at California State University,
San Francisco.

Social History/Women's Studies   £6.95
ISBN: 0 7043 3977 3

Jan Bradshaw & Mary Hemming, editors
Girls Next Door

Lesbian feminist stories
Introduced by Alison Hennegan

Eleanor discovers an unexpected love affair in her late aunt's
letters. Kira, a lesbian from another planet, pays a visit to Earth.
Speculation abounds when a neighbour discovers Miss Jones and
Miss Evans naked in their sitting room . . .

Witty, touching, funny, sad, some by established writers and
others by new, all these stories reflect the warmth and comfort
of the feeling of women for each other . . .

Fiction   £3.95
ISBN: 0 7043 3980 3
Hardcover   £7.95
ISBN: 0 7043 2871 2

Anna Livia
Accommodation Offered

' "There is a woman in Stockwell sinning," insisted Quercus.
"What's her sin?"
"Despair," said Quercus squeamishly.
"She has been ironing now for three hours, satin sheets of
oyster cream . . ." '
When Polly advertises two vacant rooms in her South London
home, Kim and Sadie move in: bus conductor Kim, and
awkward, gangling Sadie. Tensions develop as the differences
between the three women, their diverse backgrounds and
politics as lesbians, begin to divide them. Fortunately the
household is watched over by the Liberty Boddesses of Hortus,
prepared to risk even divine censure and banishment if they can
help . . .

As all who enjoyed her first novel, *Relatively Norma*, will know,
Anna Livia's is a unique voice and her style a special blend of
humour and seriousness.

Fiction   £3.95
ISBN: 0 7043 3951 X
Hardcover   £7.95
ISBN: 0 7043 2857 7

Caeia March
Three Ply Yarn

'The blitz on the London docks got my mum. My dad died in
Burma. That's when Dora and me first took to cuddling. Behind
the hay barn, while Nellie collected eggs.'

This passionate story is narrated by three women, Dee, Lotte
and Esther, as they struggle to take command of their own lives
in a world they have not made.

The three choose different paths. Lotte marries for money,
Esther seeks education and politics, Dee loves women and
learns, through her relationship with her lover's black daughter,
about an oppression different from her own. Yet their lives
increasingly intertwine, and their realisation grows of the
importance of other women to each of them.

Full of the realities of working-class lesbian experience, *Three
Ply Yarn* is an absorbing read from an important new writer.

Fiction   £3.95
ISBN: 0 7043 4007 0
Hardcover   £8.95
ISBN: 0 7043 5003 3

Suniti Namjoshi
The Conversations of Cow

Suniti and Bhadravati disagree about almost everything – which is hardly surprising as Suniti is an average middle of the road lesbian separatist and Bhadravati is a Brahmin lesbian cow, goddess of a thousand faces and a thousand manifestations.

Suniti has been unlucky in love and thinks she is becoming a misogynist. So it's only natural that when Bhadravati transforms herself into a woman, Suniti decides to become a goldfish (or perhaps a poodle or another cow). When Bhadravati manifests herself as a man, things can only get worse.

Fiction   £2.95
ISBN: 0 7043 3979 X
Hardcover   £7.95
ISBN: 0 7043 2870 4